CHASTITY AS AUTONOMY
Women in the Stories of Apocryphal Acts

VIRGINIA BURRUS

Studies in Women and Religion
Volume 23

The Edwin Mellen Press
Lewiston/Queenston

Library of Congress-in-Publication Data

Burrus, Virginia.
  Chastity as Autonomy

  (Studies in women and religion ; v. 23)
  Bibliography: p.
  Includes index.
  1. Apocryphal Acts of the Apostles--Criticism, inter-
pretation, etc. 2.Women in Christianity--History--
Early church, ca. 30-600. 3. Celibacy--Christianity--
History of doctrines--Early church, ca. 30-600. I. Title.
II. Series.
BS2871.B87 1987   229'.92067   87-7949
ISBN 0-88946-526-6

This is volume 23 in the continuing series
Studies in Women and Religion
Volume 23 ISBN 0-88946-526-6
SWR Series ISBN 0-88946-549-5

The Edwin Mellen Press   The Edwin Mellen Press
Box 450   Box 67
Lewiston, New York   Queenston, Ontario
USA 14092   CANADA L0S 1L0

Printed in the United States of America

For Karen

ACKNOWLEDGEMENTS

This monograph was originally written as a master's thesis at the Graduate Theological Union in Berkeley, California. Special thanks are due to Professors Antoinette Wire, Mary Ann Donovan, and William Herzog, who served on my thesis committee, and to University of California folklorist Alan Dundes, who patiently guided me through the intricacies of a discipline which was new to me. Dennis MacDonald and Elizabeth Clark both read the manuscript; their support and critiques were invaluable. Finally, I am deeply grateful to Bob Kelly for his constant encouragement and confidence in my project.

TABLE OF CONTENTS

Introduction   1

I. Literature or Folklore? A Review of Scholarship   7

II. A Folkloristic Analysis of the Chastity Stories:
    Identity and Structure   31

III. The Chastity Stories' Tellers   67

IV. A Social-Historical Interpretation of the Stories   81

Conclusion   113

Appendix: Summmaries of the Chastity Stories   121

Bibliography   131

Index   135

INTRODUCTION

Agrippina, Nicaria, Euphemia, and Doris go together to hear Peter preach in Rome; in response to his words, they decide to end their sexual relations with the prefect Agrippa. When Agrippa subsequently "molests" them, they take "courage to suffer every injury from Agrippa, [wishing] only to be vexed by passion no longer, beings strengthened by the power of Jesus."[1] At the same time, Xanthippe, another prominent Roman woman, also hears Peter preach and decides to separate from her husband Albinus. "Raging like a wild beast,"[2] Albinus joins with Agrippa in persecuting and eventually crucifying the preacher Peter; but the five women remain untouched and unmoved in their faith and chastity.

Maximilla of Patrae hears the apostle Andrew preach, and she too responds with a vow to live chastely. Her rejected husband, the proconsul Aegeates, crucifies Andrew but is unable to convince Maximilla to return to him. "Aegeates urged her strongly, promising her that she would have control over his affairs, but he was not able to persuade her."[3]

Thecla of Iconium is a young virgin, and when she hears the apostle Paul preach she immediately resolves not to marry. Her enraged fiance Thamyris and would-be suitor Alexander each stir up political persecution of Thecla as well as of Paul. Thecla twice faces a public execution, but on both occasions God miraculously rescues her from death, and the political authorities are forced to allow her to go free. She lives out her chaste life as a wandering Christian preacher.

These and other similar stories are found in the late second- and early third-century apocryphal Acts. In all the stories, women's chastity[4] is of central importance and is presented primarily in terms of its social consequences. Chastity leads to autonomy, freedom from the oppressive authority of husband and political ruler; it thus also leads to strong opposition on the part of these male authorities. But the women are never overcome by their opposition, however formidable, for the God who calls them to chastity also empowers them to endure all forms of persecution without relinquishing that chastity. Confident and defiant, the women are moved neither by threats of physical punishment nor by pleadings of love. And they triumph.

This presentation of women's chastity is less well-known than are the treatises on the same subject written by the "Church Fathers." It offers a picture which is strikingly inconsistent with the common assessment of early Christian women's chastity as a controlling restriction imposed on women by men. Indeed, the stories point to the possibility that the success of early Christian men in controlling and restricting women has been overestimated, perhaps due to the androcentric orientation of most of our written sources. These sources tend to define the significance of women's chastity in terms of men's actions and concerns, thus automatically implying a passive role for women; they are also often prescriptive rather than descriptive, revealing more about how men wanted women to live and think than about women's actual life styles and thoughts. The stories of the apocryphal Acts, in contrast, depict women's chastity in terms of women's actions and concerns. They appear to offer a rare glimpse of a woman's point of view.

Unfortunately, historical evaluation of the apocryphal stories is difficult. Are they to be interpreted literally as historical descriptions? Few today would take this stance. Are they descriptions of types of historical events which have been applied to non-historical characters? Or are they pure fiction or fantasy? Whose "history" or "fantasy" do these stories represent--can we in fact identify them as "women's stories"? What is their social function? And how do these last two factors affect our historical evaluation?

Most of these questions must be addressed in the interpretation of any historical text, but because the stories of the apocryphal Acts seem to include as much fantasy as fact, the methodological issues become particularly important as well as particularly complex. Many historians have preferred not to consider the stories at all, believing it to be impossible to extract clear historical information from such uncertain sources. However, to some extent it is precisely their "non-historical" nature which makes these texts valuable to students of women's history. Women have not often been history writers, and "history" has generally overlooked the lives of women. But women seem always to have been storytellers, and stories told in antiquity may provide a rich source for the reconstruction of the history of women.

This present work represents an attempt to develop a methodology for the historical interpretation of stories and to employ this methodology in the analysis of seven stories from the five earliest apocryphal Acts:[5]   the stories of Agrippina, Nicaria, Euphemia, Doris and Xanthippe (*Acts of Peter*); Maximilla (*Acts of Andrew*); Drusiana (*Acts of John*); Thecla (*Acts of Paul*); Artemilla and Eubula (*Acts of Paul*); the "princess bride" (*Acts of Thomas*); and Mygdonia and Tertia (*Acts of Thomas*). The first task will be to demonstrate that these stories are most appropriately viewed as folk-stories which were originally told by women and which reflect significant social and psychological factors of these women's experience and outlook (Chapters I-III). We will then analyze these social and psychological factors more fully, attempting to sketch in the historical background of the women's lives and struggles and thus to complement and correct androcentric portrayals of early Christian women's chastity (Chapter IV).

Notes

[1] *Acts of Peter*, E. Hennecke, *New Testament Apocrypha*, vol. 2, ed. W. Schneemelcher, Eng. trans. ed. R. McL. Wilson (London: Lutterworth Press, 1965), pp. 316-17.

[2] *Acts of Peter*, ibid., p. 317.

[3] *Acts of Andrew*, ibid., p. 423.

[4] In this work, the term "chastity" will generally be used to denote women's abstinence from all sexual relations, *not* their abstinence from extra-marital sexual relations alone. Despite the confusion which may result from this slightly unconventional use of the word "chastity" ("continence" or "celibacy," for example, might have been less ambiguous), I have chosen it for its power to evoke stereotypes of "womanly virtue."   Chastity (*sophrosyne*, *pudicitia*) is the virtue most often cited by Greek and Roman men in their praises of women. It encompasses discretion, sobriety, and diligence, but is exemplified most typically and completely through a woman's exercise of self-control in the area of sexuality. Ironically, this virtue of chastity, which is most often seen as a buttress of marital life, is precisely what enables the women in the stories of the apocryphal Acts to break out of their marriages. From the point of view of patriarchal marriage, "chastity" is thus subverted. It becomes a means not to women's restriction or subjugation but to women's autonomy.

[5] See Appendix for summaries of each of these stories and for references to their translations in Hennecke. Greek and Latin texts may be found in *Acta Apostolorum Apocrypha*, ed. R. A. Lipsius and M. Bonnet, 2 vols. (Hildesheim: Georg Olms Verlagsbuchhandlung, 1959).   Reconstruction of the text of the *Acts of Andrew* is still underway; an important recension of the story of Andrew and Maximilla not found in Lipsius and Bonnet has been published by Theodore Detorakis in *Acts of the Second International Congress of Peloponnesian Studies* I (Athens, 1981-82), pp. 333-352. See also the stories of Nicanora and Charitine in the *Acts of Philip*; the story of Trophima in Gregory of Tours' *Liber*

de Miraculis Beati Andreae Apostoli; and the *Acts of Xanthippe and Polyxena*. These are slightly later versions of the same type of story upon which this study focuses.

I. LITERATURE OR FOLKLORE? A REVIEW OF SCHOLARSHIP

Tertullian, writing at the end of the second century, attributes the *Acts of Paul* to the pen of an unnamed Asian presbyter.[1]   According to Photius, ninth-century patriarch of Constantinople, the apocryphal *Acts of Peter, John, Andrew, Thomas,* and *Paul* were written by a certain Leucius Charinus.[2] Modern scholars have not accepted the testimony of Tertullian and Photius uncritically; however, most have followed their ancient predecessors in assuming that the stories of the apocryphal Acts were the literary creations of a few male authors.[3] The widespread acceptance of this theory of literary origins necessitates not only a careful defense of any claim of folklore origins but also a critical consideration of the history of scholarship. Has past scholarship in fact demonstrated conclusively that the stories of the apocryphal Acts originated as works of literature?

History of Scholarship

Modern theories about the literary origins of the apocryphal Acts arose within the context of the study of Hellenistic literary genres.[4] The discussion of the apocryphal Acts' literary form was initiated in part by a book which had nothing directly to do with the Acts: Erwin Rohde's *Der griechische Roman*,[5] published originally in 1876.   In this lengthy work, Rohde undertakes a search for the origins of the Hellenistic romantic novel. He conducts a detailed investigation of Hellenistic erotic poetry and fabulous travel tales, which he identifies as the ancestors of the novel, and of the rhetorical schools of the "second sophistic" movement, which he regards as the birthplace of the novel.

In 1902, two years after the second edition of Rohde's work appeared, Ernst von Dobschütz[6] presented the thesis that the apocryphal Acts belong to the literary genre of the Hellenistic romantic novel. According to von Dobschütz, second-century Christianity perceived the contemporary Hellenistic novel as a literary form which it could use effectively "in the service of its propaganda":[7]

> So Christianity found the novel. The novel found Christianity. One might expect that it [the novel] reached greedily to replace its old, used-up motifs with new material. Yet one cannot say that the novel took up Christianity; rather, Christianity empowered itself with the novel.[8]

In his brief monograph, von Dobschütz identifies similarities between the novel and the Christian works primarily in the travel motif and in the interest in the exotic and the miraculous. He also emphasizes the common "love theme":

> All of these related elements would not yet justify classifying the apocryphal Acts as Greek novels if their major element, the love story, were missing. It is not the primary emphasis, as we have seen. But it is not altogether absent; it simply reveals itself to us in changed form. The erotic has here been transformed into the ascetic.[9]

Von Dobschütz' observation of the similarities between Acts and novel rightly called attention to the importance of placing Christian literature within its Hellenistic context. However, his analysis of literary genre lacked precision. He did not distinguish clearly between such differing works as the Pseudo-Clementine writings, the *Acts of Thomas*, and the fabulous *Acts of Andrew and Matthew*; nor, relying on Rohde, did he fully acknowledge the distinction between travel tales and the romantic novel.

Just a few years after the publication of von Dobschütz' monograph, Richard Reitzenstein, while working with the *Acts of Thomas*, challenged von Dobschütz' conclusion about the origin and genre of the apocryphal Acts. According to Reitzenstein, the apocryphal Acts derived not from the romantic novel but from the Hellenistic miracle story. The genre of miracle story had originated in the folk religion of Egypt before migrating to Greece and Rome, where it took the literary form of prophet and philosopher aretologies. It was these prophet and philosopher aretologies which, claimed Reitzenstein, provided the direct model for the apocryphal Acts.[10]

In his *Hellenistische Wundererzählungen*, Reitzenstein observes that the false identification of the apocryphal Acts with the romantic novel arises out of a misunderstanding of the nature of the novel.[11] Reitzenstein sets out to correct this misunderstanding by undertaking a thorough and careful analysis of the ancient narrative genres. He takes the ancient theories of rhetoric as the starting point of his analysis, hoping thereby to avoid the false imposition of modern categories of literature. The study of the ancient theories of genre is complicated by the fact that the genre we know as the "romantic novel" is not clearly referred to by any of the ancient rhetoricians, who base their generic categories on analysis of more traditional literary works. The modern confusion as to the nature and identity of the Hellenistic novel thus appears to have its roots in antiquity. However, the case is not entirely hopeless; though no ancient writer ever explicitly mentions the novel, Reitzenstein detects in the writings of Cicero an awareness of and attempt--albeit ambiguous--to define the novelistic genre.

Cicero's classification of the narrative genres, which closely parallels that found in other sources,[12] is as follows:

    1. Narratives about events (*negotia*)
        a) Myth (*fabula*)--not true or truth-like
           example: tragedy
        b) History (*historia*)--true
           example: historical epic
        c) Fiction (*argumentum*)--not true but truth-like
           example: comedy
    2. Narratives about people (*personae*)

Cicero gives little description of the three types of "narratives about events" beyond the designation of their "truth claim"; presumably, the genres of tragedy, history, and comedy are so well-known as to require no explanation. But he goes into some detail in describing the "narratives about people":

> The narrative about people is the kind in which people's speech and characters as well as their actual affairs can be examined, in this manner .... [A speech from comedy with narrative introduction follows]. This kind of narrative ought to contain much liveliness, resulting from the variety of circumstances, dissimilarity of characters, seriousness, lightness, hope, dread, suspicion, desire, dissimulation, error, pity, change of fortune, unexpected trouble, sudden joy, and the pleasant conclusion of things. (Cicero, *De Inv.* I 27)[13]

Reitzenstein suggests that Cicero is here offering a description of a "new," drama-influenced genre to which the romantic novel belongs. This genre includes the historical monograph as well; Reitzenstein points to the striking similarity between the above description of the "narrative about people" and the description of the historical monograph found in Cicero's letter to Lucceius (*Ep.* V 12). In that letter, Cicero requests that Lucceius write a history which would be separate from those "continuous histories" encompassing an endless succession of exploits which Lucceius is accus-

tomed to write. This history would instead focus on a single subject and person and come to a notable conclusion; it would be of
limited scope, but within that scope would contain as much em-
bellishment and as many twists of plot and reversals of fortune as
possible; finally, it would seek to evoke emotion, above all the
emotion of pity, and thereby to amuse and delight the reader.

> For the chronicle of historical events in itself interests us
> as little as if it were a list of calendar dates; but the un-
> certain and often changing experiences of an eminent
> man give scope for wonder, suspense, joy, trouble, hope,
> fear; if indeed they are concluded with a remarkable
> ending, the soul is filled with the most pleasant delight of
> reading. (Cicero, *Ep.* V 12.5)[14]

The historical monograph which Cicero requests of Lucceius is not,
strictly speaking, "fictional"; however, for Cicero, its highly developed dramatic form and its intention to "delight" link it with the
fictional novel in the genre of "narratives about people." [15]

Having analyzed Cicero's classification of literary genres,
Reitzenstein uses it to make the distinction between the two types
of literature which von Dobschütz had wrongly confused: the
aretology (which includes the apocryphal Acts) and the novel. Following the ancient rhetoricians, he bases the distinction on both
the "truth claim" and the literary form of these works. The aretology, with its roots in folk religion, is in origin "true history" and
even the most artful (such as Philostratos') and the parodied (such
as Lucian's) versions of the aretology imitate the simple form and
style of "history": the "acts" (*praxeis*) are presented in chronologi-
cal order with no internal connection to one another, strung like
beads on a necklace; the excitement of the narrative is produced
by the amazement which each act evokes in the reader. The novel,
on the other hand, is in origin a fictional "narrative about people."
The novel's content is artfully selected and arranged, focused on a
unified subject, with all events interwoven into a single overarching

plot; the excitement of the story builds to a single climax, which evokes a strong emotional response in the reader. Thus the complex form as well as the fictional nature of the novel distinguishes it clearly from the apocryphal Acts, which retain the formal simplicity and religious "truthfulness" of the cultically grounded aretology.[16]

Reitzenstein's interest in the possible cultic origins of the genre of the apocryphal Acts was shared by other scholars of the Religionsgeschichte school. Not all, however, were convinced that the Acts were unrelated to the novel; nor was there unanimous agreement that analysis of literary genre was the key to interpreting the origin of either Acts or novel. Scholars after Reitzenstein sought to distinguish more sharply between the folk and literary traditions which had shaped Hellenistic literature, and they turned their attention toward folklore. Reitzenstein had posited a folk origin for the aretological genre in general and perhaps also for the apocryphal Acts in particular; however, the focus of his analysis of the Acts and novel had been on the *literary* form of these works. Ludwig Rademacher and Karl Kerenyi, writing a few years later, sought instead to get at the *folklore* forms which they were convinced lay behind the literary works. Their primary methodology was comparative, and their primary goal the uncovering of origins and archetypal patterns--which they tended to equate.

Rademacher and Kerenyi each produced significant studies which attributed folkloric origins to both the apocryphal Acts and the romantic novel. In his 1916 monograph *Hippolytos und Thekla*,[17] Rademacher traces the various versions of the Hippolytus story which appear throughout the literature of ancient Greece, Thrace, and Asia Minor. He finds echoes of this story in both the Hellenistic romantic novel (Heliodorus' *Ethiopian Story* in particular) and in the story of Thecla, found in the apocryphal *Acts of Paul*. Reitzenstein concludes that the Hippolytus-Thecla story type is a wandering folk-story ultimately derived from the story of the mother earth goddess; he identifies the Hippolytus-Thecla story--somewhat vaguely--as belonging to the folk genre of "myth," "cultic legend," or "novelle."[18]

Kerenyi,[19] writing in 1927, not only utilized folkloric methods but also clearly articulated his break with the literary methods of his predecessors. In *Die griechische-orientalische Romanliteratur*, Kerenyi argues that scholarly studies of the novel and other related forms of Hellenistic literature must abandon literary analysis and pursue new questions:

> After the appearance of Rohde's book, scholarship directed its attention primarily to the formal side of the Greek novel. Now it is precisely the proven results of *this* scholarship which demonstrate the necessity of our asking the question about the origin of the novel. It showed, namely, that from the formal side there is nothing at all to be found in the Greek novel which is unique to it.... If we want to learn something about the particular essence of the Greek novel we must push beyond the form to the content, or, put historically: if the question of *origins* is important to us, we must ask it as we have just asked it.[20]

Kerenyi makes the crucial distinction between literary form and content. Whereas Reitzenstein assumes that content and genre are interrelated, Kerenyi maintains that the basic story of the novel exists independently of and prior to the novelistic form. Reitzenstein's careful analysis of the literary genre of the novel does not therefore necessarily tell us anything about the origin or the nature of its basic story. Indeed, insofar as scholars demonstrate that the literary genre of the novel is purely derivative from other genres (such as erotic poetry or drama) they show that its literary characteristics are not its essential or distinguishing characteristics.

In separating literary genre from story, Kerenyi also separates the truth claims of that genre from the story. He maintains that the novel's story was not originally fictional, but fell into the category of myth. To explain how myth came to be taken up into a fictional genre, Kerenyi notes that in the Hellenistic period educated Greeks had come to identify religious myth with lie; they emphasized the distinction between fiction and lie in an effort to avoid and condemn myth. It was only in this context that the authors of the novels wanted their mythical stories to be understood as "fiction," and they made every effort to present it as such, especially by offering rational explanations for seeming miracles. They also used a second legitimizing tactic: they tried to associate their works with the classical literary genres which were the only acceptable form of myth, the idyllic (exemplified in Longus' novel), the erotic (exemplified in Achilles Tatius' novel), and the tragic-heroic (exemplified in Heliodorus' novel).[21]

Like von Dobschütz and Rademacher, Kerenyi relates the novel to popular Christian literature; like Rademacher and unlike von Dobschütz, he views them not as literarily dependent but as different literary versions of the same non-literary story. Of particular interest is his discussion of eroticism in the novel and in Christian literature. Here Kerenyi focuses not on the apocryphal Acts but on other popular Christian literature where the theme of "threatened and victoriously defended chastity" also appears. He notes that there is at least one story treatment of this theme which can be traced back as far as the first century B.C.E., where it appears in the elder Seneca's collection of controversies:[22] this is the story of the chaste young woman who is forced into prostitution, yet successfully resists all attempts to defile her purity. In addition to the elder Seneca's version, this story is found in Xenophon's novel and in several Christian martyrdom accounts. The repetitious versions and the ease with which the story is transferred

from one setting to another show clearly that it is neither a historical account nor an original fiction but a legend.[23]

In this story as in others centering around the same
theme of chastity threatened and defended, Kerenyi detects a puz-
zling juxtaposition of exaggerated emphases on both sexuality and
chastity. In seeking to explain this puzzle, he notes that virginity
and chastity are not equivalent, and that virginity is emphasized
only in the latest novelistic versions of the erotic story. Furthermore, in at least three versions of the erotic story,[24] the heroine is
actually pregnant when she undergoes the threats to her
chastity.[25] It is this pregnancy which offers Kerenyi the clue to the
story's origins in cultic myth, for it recalls the stories of Io and Isis.
Kerenyi particularly develops the parallels with the story of Io.
After having sexual intercourse with Zeus, Io is changed into a
heifer, in which form she is persecuted by Hera, who sends a gad-
fly to torture her. Driven mad by the insect, Io wanders all over
the world until she reaches Egypt. There Zeus restores her to
human form, and she bears a child. Curiously, Io is referred to as
a "virgin shunning the love of man,"[26] even after her intercourse
with Zeus. To explain this designation, Kerenyi points to a study
by Eugen Fehrle[27] which demonstrates that the ancient Greeks believed that a woman honored by sexual intercourse with a god
must forgo the love of a man. The notion of the importance of the
chastity of the "Gottesbraut" helps explain not only the reference to
the pregnant Io as "virgin" but also the seemingly conflicting emphases of the novelistic love story, which always begins with a
highly erotic scene but thereafter focuses on the heroine's chastity.
In Kerenyi's view, the heroine of the novel and of the related Christian stories is in her origins a "Gottesbraut," one whose sexuality
and chastity are both highly significant.[28] The novelistic story, if
not the literary genre, has its roots in religious myth.

In 1932, thirty years after the initiation of the discussion
by von Dobschütz, Rosa Söder[29] published a study focusing

specifically on the relationship of the apocryphal Acts to the various forms of the Hellenistic novel. While she avoided the excesses of the theories of Rademacher and Kerenyi--who had sometimes been overly quick to relate stories or to identify cultic roots--she shared their interest in folklore and attempted in her work to draw together both the literary and folkloric strands of the discussion of the apocryphal Acts.

In *Die apokryphen Apostelgeschichten und die romanhafte Literatur der Antike*, Söder defines the term "novel" broadly to include not only the romantic novel studied by von Dobschütz but also the historical, philosphical and comical novels which scholars like Reitzenstein had proven also possessed striking similarities to the apocryphal Acts. Söder, like Kerenyi, avoids using the term "novel" to designate a literary *genre*; instead, she conceives of the novel as a general body of Hellenistic literature which is characterized by the use of several thematic "elements." She identifies five essential novelistic elements: (1) the element of travel; (2) the aretological element; (3) the teratological element (descriptions of fabulous or exotic people, animals, or events); (4) the tendentious element; and (5) the erotic element. Söder examines the apocryphal Acts to find out whether they contain these five elements, and, upon discovering that they do, concludes that the apocryphal Acts should indeed be included in the general category of the Hellenistic novel.[30]

Söder does not dispense altogether with the concept of literary genre, but continues to observe the traditional distinction between genres within the general category of novelistic literature. She questions whether the apocryphal Acts show an especially close relationship to any one of these genres. Here she conducts her analysis on the basis not only of the five "main elements" but also of five additional "special motifs" found in the apocryphal Acts: (1) sale into slavery; (2) persecution; (3) crowds; (4) divine help in great need; and (5) oracles, dreams, and divine commands. Her survey of the apocryphal Acts and the various genres of Hellenistic novel with attention to these elements and motifs suggest that the apocryphal Acts cannot be identified with any one novelistic genre. Contrary to Reitzenstein's thesis, the Acts cannot be identified with the aretology, because the aretology lacks not only the element of eroticism but most of the special motifs as well, whereas the apocryphal Acts contain all of these.[31]

The romantic novel appears to be a better candidate, for it shares with the apocryphal Acts most of the main elements and special motifs. However, the teratological and aretological elements are missing from the novel, and there are also significant differences between the eroticism of the novel and that of the Acts; indeed, to some extent eroticism is replaced by asceticism in the apocryphal Acts, as von Dobschütz pointed out. Söder acknowledges that the relationship between the woman and the apostle does contain erotic overtones, and notes that there are a number of erotic motifs in the apocryphal Acts which have close parallels in the Hellenistic romantic novel:

> constant mention of beauty; love at first sight; rejection of those who have prior claim; change of clothes; the abandoned one's jealousy and laments; visits in prison with attempted bribery of the guard; the motif of scorned love which changes into hate and vents itself (a) against the one formerly loved, (b) against the rival; the motif of delay and evasion; steadfastness against suitors, threats, and even against brutal force; faithful slaves; etc.[32]

But the existence of these shared motifs need not indicate direct relationship between the romantic novel and the apocryphal Acts; most of them are common to fairy tales and folk narratives as well. And the omission of the teratological and aretological elements in the romantic novel speaks out strongly against such a direct relationship.[33]

Thus, the apocryphal Acts cannot be identified with any single Hellenistic literary genre; but neither do they seem to represent a simple blending of aretology and romantic novel, for they are related to several other literary and folk genres as well: "the Ionian novelle, the Greek cycle of myths, Hellenistic mysticism, old legends and fairy tales and earthy folk humor, and, as Reitzenstein believes, even Egyptian magic and miracle tales."[34]   How is one to explain the relationship of the Acts to all of these genres?   Söder notes that it would not have been absolutely unprecedented for Christianity to have "created a new literary form out of the most diverse elements."[35]   However, if that were the case, literary dependence among the apocryphal Acts would have to be assumed.   She finds no clear evidence for such literary dependence.

Söder believes that the answer to the question of the relationship of the Acts to other genres lies in a consideration of their purpose, which is to offer edification in an entertaining and easily comprehensible form.   Consistent with this purpose is the retention of folk elements.   Though the authors were clearly also familiar with more sophisticated literary genres, which shape the outer form of their works, Söder maintains that folk narratives were the primary source for their stories and motifs.   Like Rademacher and Kerenyi, she finds that mutual dependence on a common non-literary source is the best explanation for the similarities between Hellenistic novel and Christian literature.

> . . . A work of literature must not always be the direct development of an immediately preceding or contemporary known genre with which it shows similarity and agreement; they can both also come out of a common source unknown to us.
>
> And so I view the apocryphal Acts as the literarily fixed (and indeed, fixed in the Christian Spirit) *witnesses of ancient folk stories* of the adventures, miraculous deeds, and love affairs of great men--whether they owe their real

or invented life to history or myth or even the fantasy of the people. But if this is so, then the apocryphal Acts win a greater meaning for the history of the novel in general, as well as the Hellenistic novel in particular, as witnesses of a form which would otherwise have been lost to us, since it does not belong to literature, and out of which all the similar kinds could develop.[36]

Söder's identification of the apocryphal Acts as folk-stories thinly veiled in literary form is reminiscent of Reitzenstein's claim that the Acts represent that literary form of the aretology which lies closest to its hypothesized folk original. And clearly her conclusion is in harmony with the basic thesis of both Rademacher and Kerenyi: the stories and motifs of the Hellenistic novelistic literature, including the Acts, are of folkloric origin. It might seem that with Söder's monograph some agreement concerning the origin and nature of the apocryphal Acts had been reached. This was the opinion of Schneemelcher and Schäferdiek, who accepted Söder's conclusions as a "firm basis for a proper comprehension of the apocryphal Acts, on which further work can proceed."[37] But recent scholarship has been more critical of Söder's work.

Philipp Vielhauer[38] agrees with Söder that the apocryphal Acts exhibit close parallels with the "novelistic literature of antiquity" and also possess many folk motifs which betray their relationship to both cultic legend and novelle.[39] However, he questions Söder's basic method of characterizing literary genres in terms of a collection of content-related motifs as well as her conclusion that the apocryphal Acts are not to be identified with any single novelistic genre. Vielhauer himself defines genre in terms of form rather than content. He believes that the form of the apocryphal Acts evolved out of the traditional aretological acts (*praxeis*) and travel narratives (*periodoi*): while the acts provided the primary structure, the travel narrative was superimposed on this structure, serving to tie the individual acts together. This melding of acts and travel narrative produced the literary genre of "travel novel." The "travel novel" (much like Söder's general category of "novel") embraces a variety of types, including "historical" and "romantic" novels, which both appear to have influenced the apocryphal Acts significantly.   Vielhauer disagrees with Söder that these "types" should be viewed as separate "genres." The formal unity of the apocryphal Acts, romantic novel, and other forms of the "travel novel" identify them as a single genre. Nor is Vielhauer convinced by Söder's argument that the apocryphal Acts and novel represent different "levels" of literature and should therefore be viewed as separate genres. The apocryphal Acts are not as primitive, nor the novel as sophisticated as she suggests; both seek to appeal to a broad audience.[40]

In some respects, Vielhauer's disagreement with Söder appears to be superficial, particularly as regards his objection to her use of the word "genre." It is not clear that Söder--or even Kerenyi--would disagree that the apocryphal Acts have in part been shaped by the literary structures which Vielhauer identifies with those of the "travel novel." But the fact that Vielhauer prefers to emphasize the importance of those literary structures at the expense of the folklore forms and motifs which Söder finds so significant reflects Söder's failure to demonstrate convincingly the existence of the Acts' folk antecedents. It is likely that most of the "elements" and "motifs" which Söder identifies are indeed of folklore origin; their frequent repetition within Hellenistic literature and the fluidity with which they move from one work to another suggest this, and comparison with known folklore sources might confirm it. But Söder is not claiming merely that the apocryphal Acts contain folk motifs, but further that the apocryphal stories themselves are folk-stories. Because Söder fails to offer analysis or comparison of narrative structure beyond the level of "element" or "motif," her folk-stories remain purely hypothetical, and her literary genres formless.

Jean-Daniel Kaestli joins Vielhauer in expressing dissatisfaction with Söder's method of "defining what belongs to a literary genre by adding up certain thematic characteristics."[41] He furthermore points out the inconsistency in Söder's choice of "elements": of the five main elements, four relate to thematic content, while the fifth, the "tendentious element," has to do with the general doctrinal and moral intention of the text.[42] Kaestli, like Vielhauer, prefers to limit his consideration to a more traditional analysis of literary genre. Avoiding the oversimplicity of von Dobschütz' theory, he concedes that the romantic novel cannot have been the *only* literary model for the apocryphal Acts; indeed, the apocryphal Acts appear to him to be "an original creation of Christianity, born of the combination of diverse literary influences."[43] Nevertheless, Kaestli maintains that "those stories of the apocryphal Acts where the erotic theme predominates are directly inspired by the genre of the Hellenistic romantic novel,"[44] and he particularly challenges Söder's grounds for denying this. "Can the frequency and the closeness of the parallels be explained otherwise than by a direct influence of the Hellenistic romantic novel on the apocryphal Acts?"[45] He believes that Söder's judgment to the contrary is based not only on her faulty methodology of genre definition but also on two misconceptions about the novel.

First, Söder erroneously follows Rohde in dating the novel late, in the period of the second sophistic movement, whereas papyri discoveries since the publication of Rohde's work have revealed that the novel existed as early as the first or second century B.C.E. This early dating of the novel makes its direct influence on the apocryphal Acts even more likely. Second, Söder understands the novel to be a sophisticated literary form, whereas more recent research has indicated that the novel in its earliest phase was a popular form. Again, this factor suggests to Kaestli a greater likelihood that the novel directly influenced the apocryphal Acts-- though Söder might well challenge that the novel's lower social location *also* makes it more likely that the novel itself was based on folk material.[46]

Kaestli's return to the emphasis on the influence of the Hellenistic romantic novel on the stories about women in the apocryphal Acts is shared by other scholars who treat these stories only in passing. Paul Achtemeier views the stories as conscious adaptations of the novel for missionary purposes:

> If it is true, therefore, as seems to be the case, that the authors of the apocryphal Acts have adapted literary conventions of the Hellenistic world in the composition and structure of their narratives, and if, as seems equally to be the case, those elements make the Acts more "entertaining," and thus more likely to be read, then it would also seem to be the case that the authors had some kind of apologetic and/or missionary intention underlying their work. They appear to have wanted to gain readers for their works and were willing to cast those works in a form currently popular. To that extent, they adapted their understanding of the Christian message to the literary tastes of the second and third centuries.[47]

Similarly, Elizabeth Schussler Fiorenza finds that in the Thecla story "motifs of the Hellenistic novel or romance are here taken over for missionary purposes"; she adds that "those legends and stories could present women as preachers and missionaries only in romantic disguise."[48]   JoAnn McNamara likewise refers to the "romance called the *Acts of Paul and Thecla.*"[49]

In spite of this trend toward literary interpretations, folklore studies of the apocryphal Acts have not been entirely abandoned. With his recent publication of *The Legend and the Apostle: The Battle for Paul in Story and Canon,* Dennis MacDonald has renewed the effort to identify folklore elements in the apocryphal Acts.[50] Following the example of Rademacher, who also worked primarily with the *Acts of Paul,* MacDonald cites the existence of variant versions of the stories of the *Acts of Paul* as one proof of the folklore origins of those stories; he calls particular attention to the close parallels between the Thecla story and the roughly contemporary story of Hagnodice, the first Greek woman physician.[51] Even more significant than his discovery of parallel stories is MacDonald's analysis of the narrative technique of the *Acts of Paul*. Folklorist Alex Olrick has developed a list of "laws" of folk narrative, which describe the conventions or tendencies of oral storytelling; these include the law of opening, the law of concentration on a leading character, the law of contrast, the law of twins, the law of the single strand, the law of repetition, the use of tableaux scenes, and the law of closing;[52] to this list MacDonald adds the law of narrative inconsistencies which has been observed by folklorist Albert B. Lord.[53] MacDonald discovers that a number of the stories in the *Acts of Paul* follow these "laws" closely, indicating that they have not only been borrowed from oral traditions but have also been left largely in their oral form. Utilizing the results of folklore scholarship, MacDonald thus places the discussion of the folklore origins of at least one of the apocryphal Acts on a much firmer footing. By focusing on the contemporary social and cultural conditions which shaped the oral legends about Paul and Thecla--rather than attempting to explain these legends as variants of an "earth goddess" or "god's bride" myth--MacDonald also points a new direction for the interpretation of the folkloric stories.

Summary and Conclusions

In 1902 Ernst von Dobschütz set forth the thesis that the apocryphal Acts were literary creations modelled on the Hellenistic romantic novel. In subsequent years, attempts were made to prove the Acts' relationship to other Hellenistic literary genres as well as to various folk traditions. Rosa Söder in 1932 presented the thesis that both the apocryphal Acts and the novel were based on folk traditions; a reliance on common traditions accounted for similarities between the two bodies of literature. Though Söder's work was extremely influential, her conclusions were not universally accepted. In recent scholarship, the influence of folklore on the Acts has not been completely ruled out; however, literary analysis is preferred by most scholars, possibly because they find that clear and persuasive evidence of folklore origins has not yet been presented. This "preference" for analysis of the literary genre of the apocryphal Acts, combined with a tendency to confuse genre with origin, has resulted in a widespread view that the apocryphal Acts were in their origin self-conscious literary creations modelled primarily on the Hellenistic romantic novel. There has thus been a return to the original theory of von Dobschütz, though this theory is now applied more precisely to the apocryphal stories about women rather than to the Acts as a whole.

There are two major problems with the view that the apocryphal Acts are essentially romantic novels. First, it ignores the considerable evidence of folklore motifs and narratives in the apocryphal Acts. However imperfect their methods and conclusions may appear in retrospect, scholars like Rademacher, Kerenyi, and Söder have clearly demonstrated that folklore informed the apocryphal Acts and perhaps also the novel in significant ways; the nature and extent of its influence still remains to be explored more thoroughly. Second, it is surely a mistake to equate the identification of the literary genre of the Acts with the identification of their origin. It is possible that the apocryphal Acts are indeed "Christian novels"; that is to say, their literary form may be both similar to and derived from the genre of the romantic novel. However, what does their identification as "novels" really tell us about the origins of the apocryphal Acts? What, in the words of Ben Edwin Perry, are "the real forces . . . that create new literary forms" like that of the apocryphal Acts?[54]

Such forms, I am convinced, never come into being as
the result of an evolutionary process taking place on the
purely literary plane, but only as the willful creations of
men made in accordance with a conscious purpose.
That purpose, in the case of the more important and well
established genres, is to satisfy the new spiritual or in-
tellectual needs and tastes that have arisen in a large
part of society in a given period of cultural history. . . .
This new thing will not be the end-product of a series of
accidents, or of successive imitations, or of rhetorical ex-
periments, or even of a gradual shifting of emphasis on
the part of those who write in a traditional and already
established form. One form does not give birth to another, but is separated from it by a logically unbridgeable
gap.[55]

Perry's words are addressed to Rohde and other scholars of the
romantic novel who have attempted to explain the origin of the
genre of the romantic novel as the "product" of other genres. They
might equally be addressed to those scholars of the apocryphal
Acts who, in their eagerness to identify the Acts with a known Hellenistic genre, have undervalued both the uniqueness of the apocryphal Acts and the significance of the contemporary social and
cultural factors which produced them.

Dennis MacDonald has reopened the question of the apocryphal Acts' folklore origins and has demonstrated the historical
value of the Acts as witnesses of the social world of the folk who
produced them. Much more research still remains to be done in
exploring the role which folklore played in the composition of the
apocryphal Acts. This present work will test the hypothesis that
the stories about women and chastity which are found in the apocryphal Acts originated as folk-stories. Folkloristic analysis of the
chastity stories will be combined with a reevaluation of the relationship of the apocryphal Acts to the literary genre of the Hel-

lenistic romantic novel. For only through an investigation of both folklore and literary aspects are we likely to acquire an accurate view of the origin and nature of the apocryphal Acts.

Notes

[1] Tertullian, *On Baptism* I.17.

[2] See W. Schneemelcher and K. Schäferdiek, "Second and Third Century Acts of Apostles: Introduction," Hennecke, *New Testament Apocrypha*, pp. 178-79.

[3] Given the paucity of known female authors in the Hellenistic world of the second century C.E., to assume "authorship" of a story is, for most scholars, to assume *male* authorship. Stevan Davies, *The Revolt of the Widows: The Social World of the Apocryphal Acts* (Carbondale and Edwardsville: Southern Illinois Univ. Press, 1980), makes a rare claim for female authorship of the Acts; however, Dennis MacDonald, "The Role of Women in the Production of the Apocryphal Acts of the Apostles," *The Illif Review* 40.4 (Winter 1984):21-38, has raised serious questions about the plausibility of Davies' claim.

[4] The discussion of literary genre is most relevant to my topic but is by no means the only area of scholarly discussion of the apocryphal Acts. See Jean-Daniel Kaestli, "Les Principales Orientations de la Recherche sur les Actes Apocryphes des Apôtres," *Les Actes apocryphes des Apôtres*, ed. F. Bovon (Geneva: Labor et fides, 1981), pp. 49-67, for an overview of the major areas of research on the apocryphal Acts; these include text criticism and theological examination as well as the study of literary genre.

[5] Erwin Rohde, *Der griechische Roman und seine Vorläufer*, 2nd ed. (Leipzig: Breitkopf und Hartel, 1900).

[6] E. von Dobschütz, "Der Roman in der altchristlichen Literatur," *Deutsche Rundschau* 111 (1902):87-106.

[7] "in den Dienst seiner Propaganda." Ibid., p. 92.

[8] "So fand das Christenthum den antiken Roman vor. Der Roman fand das Christenthum. Man dürfte erwarten, dass er statt der abgebrauchten alten Motive begierig nach dem neuen Stoffe griff. Doch kann man nicht sagen, dass der Roman das Christen-

thum aufnahm; vielmehr das Christenthum bemächtigte sich des Romans." Ibid., p. 91.

⁹ "Alle diese verwandten Elemente würden doch noch nicht berechtigen, die Apostelgeschichten den griechischen Romanen einzureihen, wenn deren Hauptmoment, die Liebesgeschichte, fehlte. Sie steht nicht an erster Stelle, das sahen wir schon. Aber sie fehlt doch nicht ganz; nur zeigt sie sich uns in verkehrter Gestalt. Die Erotik ist hier zur Asketik geworden." Ibid., p. 101.

¹⁰ Richard Reitzenstein, *Hellenistische Wundererzählungen* (Leipzig: B. G. Teubner, 1906), p. 55.

¹¹ Ibid., p. 35.

¹² See for example *Ad Herennium* I 12.13, ibid., pp. 92-3.

¹³ "Illa autem narratio, quae versatur in personis, eiusmodi est, ut in ea simul cum rebus ipsis personarum sermones et animi perspici possint, hoc modo.... Hoc in genere narrationis multa debet inesse festivitas confecta ex rerum varietate animorum dissimilitudine gravitate levitate spe metu suspicione desiderio dissimulatione errore misericordia fortunae commutatione insperato incommodo subita laetitia, iucundo exitu rerum." (Cicero, *De Inv.* I 27)

¹⁴ "At viri saepe excellentis ancipites variique casus habent admirationem exspectationem laetitiam molestiam spem timorem; si vero exitu notabili concluduntur, expletur animus iucundissima lectionis voluptate." (Cicero *Ep.* V 12.5)

¹⁵ Reitzenstein, pp. 84-94.

¹⁶ Ibid., pp. 97-8.

¹⁷ Ludwig Rademacher, "Hippolytos und Thekla. Studien zur Geschichte von Legende und Kultus," *Sitzungsberichte, Kaiserliche Akademie der Wissenschaft in Wein, Philosophisch-historische Klasse* 182.3 (Vienna, 1916).

¹⁸ Ibid., pp. 55-6, 91. Note that while the genres of myth and cultic legend are well established in current folklore theory, the folk genre of "novelle" is less clearly defined. Like the term "novel," the term "novelle" is a modern word applied anachronistically to an ancient genre. Herodotus is one of the chief witnesses of the so-called Ionian novelle, a folk "short story" which is often erotic in content. See Wolf Aly, *Volksmärchen, Sage und Novelle bei Herodot und seinen Zeitgenossen* (Göttingen: Vandenhoek und Ruprecht, 1921).

[19] Karl Kerenyi, *Die griechische-orientalische Romanliteratur in religionsgeschichtlicher Beleuchtung* (Tübingen, 1927; reprint ed., Darmstadt: Wissenschaftliche Buchgesellschaft, 1962).

[20] "Nach dem Erscheinen von Rohdes Buch richtete die Forschung ihr Augenmerk hauptsächlich auf die formale Seite des griechischen Romans. Nun sind es gerade die gesicherten Ergebnisse *dieser* Forschung, die die Notwendigkeit unserer Fragestellung zur Bestimmung der Herkunft des Romans bezeugen. Es zeigte sich nämlich, dass von der formalen Seite her im griechischen Roman überhaupt nichst zu finden ist, was ihm eigen wäre. . . . Wenn wir etwas über das eigenste Wesen des griechischen Roman erfahren möchten, so müssen wir eben vom Formellen bis zum Sachlichen vordringen, oder historisch gesprochen: wenn uns die Frage nach seinem *Ursprung* wichtig ist, so müssen wir sie so stellen, wie wir sie eben gestellt haben." Ibid., p. viii.

[21] Ibid., pp. 6-19.

[22] The Elder Seneca, *Controversia* I.2.

[23] Kerenyi, pp. 210-13.

[24] Archistratis (*History of Apollonius*), Callirhoe (Chariton's novel), and Psyche (Apuleius' novel).

[25] Kerenyi, pp. 217-18.

[26] Aeschylus, *Prometheus* 898.

[27] Eugen Fehrle, *Die kultische Keuschheit im Altertum* (Giessen, 1919 - RGVV VI), cited by Kerenyi, p. 219.

[28] Kerenyi, pp. 218-19.

[29] Rosa Söder, *Die apokryphen Apostelgeschichten und die romanhafte Literatur der Antike* (Stuttgart, 1932; reprint ed., Darmstadt: Wissenschaftliche Buchgesellschaft, 1969).

[30] Ibid., p. 181.

[31] Ibid., pp. 183-84.

[32] "ständig Erwähnung der Schönheit, Liebe auf den ersten Blick, Zurückweisung des Erstberechtigten, Kleidungswechsel, Eifersucht und Liebesklagen der Verlassenen, Besuche im Kerker mit dem Versuch zur Bestechung der Wachter; das Motiv der verschmähten Liebe, die sich in Hass wendet und sich äussert (a) gegen die frühere Geliebte, (b) gegen den Nebenbuhler; das Motiv des Aufschubs und der Ausflucht, Standhaftigkeit gegen

Schmeicheleien, Drohungen und selbst gegen brutale Gewalt, getreue Sklaven u.a.m." Ibid., p. 148.

33 Ibid., pp. 184-85.

34 "die jonische Novelle, der griechische Mythenkreis, die hellenistische Mystik, die alten Volkssagen und Märchen und urwüchsiger Volkshumor... und, wie Reitzenstein glaubt, selbst ägyptische Zauber- und Wundererzählungen." Ibid., pp. 185-86.

35 "aus den verschiedensten Elementen eine neue Literaturform geschaffen." Ibid., p. 186.

36 "Es muss ja auch ein Literaturwerk nicht immer die unmittelbare Entwicklungsstufe einer uns bekannten unmittelbar vorhergehenden oder gleichzeitigen Gattung sein, mit der es Ähnlichkeit und Übereinstimmungen zeigt, sie können beide auch aus einem gemeinsamen uns verschollenen Urquell herkommen. Und so halte ich denn die AGG als die literarisch, und zwar in christlichem Geiste fixierten *Zeugen alter im Volke lebender Erzählungen* von den Abenteuern, Wundertaten und Liebesaffären grosser Männer, mögen diese ihr wirkliches oder erdachtes Leben nun der Geschichte oder dem Mythos oder auch lediglich der Phantasie des Volkes verdanken. Ist dem aber so, dann gewinnen die AGG für die Geschichte des Romans überhaupt, wie des hellenistischen insonderheit, als Zeugen einer, weil nicht der Literatur angehörigen, sonst für uns verschollenen Form, aus der alle die ähnlichen Arten sich entwickeln konnten, erhöhte Bedeutung." Ibid., p. 187.

37 W. Schneemelcher and K. Schäferdiek, "Second and Third Century Acts of Apostles: Introduction," p. 176.

38 Philipp Vielhauer, "Apokryphe Apostelgeschichten," *Geschichte der urchristlichen Literatur* (Berlin, NY: Walter de Gruyter, 1975).

39 Ibid., p. 714.

40 Ibid., pp. 716-18.

41 "définir l'appartenance à un genre littéraire par l'addition de certaines caractéristiques thématiques." Kaestli, p. 61.

42 Ibid., p. 63.

43 "une création originale du christianisme, née de la combinaison d'influences littéraires diverses." Ibid., p. 67.

[44] "Les récits des Actes apocryphes où prédomine le thème érotique sont directement inspirés par le genre du roman d'amour hellénistique." Ibid.

[45] "La fréquence et l'étroitesse de ces parallèles peuvent-elles s'expliquer autremont que par une influence directe du roman d'amour hellénistique sur les Actes apocryphes?" Ibid., p. 66.

[46] Ibid., pp. 66-67. For recent discussions of the novel and its social setting and origins, see Tomas Hägg, *The Novel in Antiquity* (Berkeley & LA: Univ. of Cal. Press, 1983); Donald Norman Levin, "To Whom Did the Ancient Novelists Address Themselves?," *Rivista di Studi Classici* 24 (1977): 18-29; Ben Edwin Perry, *The Ancient Romances: A Literary-Historical Account of Their Origins* (Berkeley & LA: Univ. of Cal. Press, 1967); B. P. Reardon, "The Greek Novel," *Phoenix* 23 (1969): 291-309; Alexander Scobie, *Aspects of the Ancient Romance and Its Heritage* (Meisenheim am Glan: Verlag Anton Hain, 1969).

[47] Paul J. Achtemeier, "Jesus and the Disciples as Miracle Workers in the Apocryphal New Testament," *Aspects of Religious Propaganda in Judaism and Early Christianity*, ed. E. Schussler Fiorenza (Notre Dame: Univ. of Notre Dame Press, 1976), p. 104.

[48] Elizabeth Schussler Fiorenza, *In Memory of Her* (NY: Crossroad Publishing Co., 1983), p. 174.

[49] Jo Ann McNamara, *A New Song: Celibate Women in the First Three Christian Centuries* (NY: Harrington Park Press, 1985), p. 68.

[50] Dennis R. MacDonald, *The Legend and the Apostle: The Battle for Paul in Story and Canon* (Philadelphia: Westminster Press, 1983).

[51] The story of Hagnidice is found in *The Myths of Hyginus*, tr. and ed. Mary Grant (Univ. of Kansas Press, 1960), cited by MacDonald, p. 107, n.16.

[52] MacDonald, pp. 26-32. See also Alex Olrick, "Epic Laws of Folk Narrative," *The Study of Folklore*, ed. A. Dundes (Englewood Cliffs, NJ, 1965), pp. 131-41.

[53] MacDonald, pp. 32-33. See also Albert B. Lord, *The Singer of Tales* (Reprint edition: Cambridge: Harvard Univ. Press, 1978), p. 94.

[54] Perry, p. 9.

[55] Ibid., pp. 9-10.

II. A FOLKLORISTIC ANALYSIS OF THE CHASTITY STORIES: IDENTITY AND STRUCTURE

The stories about women and chastity which are found in the apocryphal Acts are folk-stories--that is the hypothesis which the present chapter sets out to test. This claim has significant implications for the study of the apocryphal Acts. In the history of scholarship it is these "chastity stories" which have most often been cited as evidence of the apocryphal Acts' *literary* origins. The stories about chaste women, it is claimed, link the apocryphal Acts with the Hellenistic romantic novel. The chastity stories have thus established the apocryphal Acts as "Christian romances"; their identification as folk-stories provides a serious challenge to this traditional view.

The claim of folklore origins for the chastity stories has significant implications for the study of women's history as well. Women in antiquity were not "well published": ancient sources attribute all of the surviving Hellenistic novels as well as the apocryphal Acts to male authors. Literary origins for the chastity stories therefore argue against their identity as women's stories. Folklore origins, on the other hand, leave open the possibility that these stories represent the voices of early Christian women.

As the history of scholarship has demonstrated, "proving" the existence of second-century oral traditions is no simple matter. Some literarily preserved stories betray probable folk origins through their use of typical oral narrative techniques (such as those identified by Olrick) or folk motifs (such as those catalogued in Thompson's *Motif-Index of Folk Literature*);[1] however, folk origins are not a certainty in such cases, since the possibility remains that the story itself is a literary creation with a strong folk influence in narrative style. Folk origins can be claimed with more confidence if a story not only conforms to the conventions of folk narrative but also exists in multiple versions, or "variants," where direct literary influence among these variants seems unlikely. Once variants of a single "tale type" have appeared over a sufficiently large span of time and space, the story may be identified conclusively as a product of oral tradition.

Identification of "types" and "variants" is sometimes difficult. First, the necessary historical and cross-cultural data is often unavailable to the scholar, particularly in the case of legends, the largest--and therefore most difficult to catalogue--of the major narrative folk genres. Second, even where sufficient data is available, it may be difficult to classify narratives accurately. A narrative may appear to be related to more than one tale type; or it may be unclear whether it should be considered a variant of an existing tale type, or the representative of a new, historically independent tale type. Rademacher and Kerenyi are criticized for having been too quick to identify extremely diverse stories as variants of a single type; their mistakes become more understandable when viewed in light of the ambiguity of the definition of the concept of a "type."

The chastity stories--if they are indeed folk-stories--are legends; that is to say, they are folk-stories which claim to present history. Comparative cross-cultural and historical data is therefore not easily available to provide "proof" of the chastity stories' folklore origins. This present study will be limited primarily to one historic-geographic location--the Hellenistic world--and to two major bodies of literature--the apocryphal Acts and the Hellenistic novel. In the absence of sufficient data documenting the historical and geographic spread of the stories, *conclusive* evidence of the chastity stories' folk origins will remain elusive. However, a comparative analysis of the stories about women and chastity can offer many insights into their *probable* origins and interrelationships.

Analysis must begin with a clear identification of the narrative structure of the chastity stories and the stories of the romantic novel; "if we are incapable of breaking the tale into its components, we will not be able to make a correct comparison."[2] A clear understanding of the stories' narrative structure will aid not only in establishing the interrelationships of the various stories and in formulating a reasonable theory about their origins, but also in understanding the distinctive meaning of the stories: identification leads naturally to interpretation.

Structure of the Chastity Story

When in the 1920's Vladimir Propp was faced with the confusion of the various attempts of folklorists to classify folkstories according to "themes" or "tale types," he remarked: "Clearcut division into types does not actually exist."[3] Propp recognized the need for an objective and consistent method for identifying narrative "types" by breaking narratives down into their fundamental components and then describing the organization of those components. According to Propp, a "function," which consists of both a "role" and an "action," was the basic component of narrative structure; a sequence of functions could be used to define a story "type." Propp used this new method of definition to analyze the narrative structure of Russian fairy tales, and he discovered that all conformed to a single, surprisingly complex narrative type, or sequence of functions. Propp concluded that "the entire store of fairy tales ought to be examined as a *chain* of variants" of a single structural type.[4] Propp found that variants of this type might omit certain of the typical functions, but they never altered the order of the sequence of functions. Roles might be filled by different characters, and actions might be carried out in different ways, but the basic functions remained constant throughout the corpus of Russian fairy tales.

The broad application of Propp's typology to all of Russian fairy tales suggested to folklorists that shared narrative structure did not necessarily indicate direct historical relationship of stories; Propp's "structural type" was not after all identical with a "tale type." Propp had created a method of describing patterns which might define an entire folk genre (i.e., the folktale) or one culturally-specific form of that genre (i.e., Russian fairy tales); it might also be used to define a group of historically dependent tales, that is, a "tale type."5 The manifold uses of Propp's method of narrative analysis are still being explored and developed by scholars today.

Proppian structural analysis can be applied with relative ease to the apocryphal stories about women and chastity and provides an objective way of defining the typical "chastity story." The following sequence of functions represents the basic narrative structure of the chastity story type, broken down into functions, each of which includes a role and an action:

1. Apostle arrives in town.
2. Woman goes to hear apostle preach.
3. Woman vows chastity.
4. Husband attempts to violate vow.
5. Apostle encourages woman.
6. Woman resists husband.
7. Husband/governor imprisons apostle.
8. Woman visits apostle in prison (encourage-ment; baptism).
9. Husband/governor attempts to kill apostle.
10. Apostle dies or is rescued (leaves the scene).
11. Husband/governor persecutes Woman.
12. Woman is rescued.

13. Woman defeats husband/governor (who may be
    converted or punished, and never succeeds in
    persuading the woman).
14. Woman is freed (allowed to remain chaste).

This structural definition of the story provides a standard by which the chastity stories may be compared. To what degree does each of the stories conform to this typical pattern? How closely related are the variants of this structural type? An examination of the chastity stories will provide the answer to these questions.[6]

(1) *The Story of Agrippina, Nicaria, Euphemia, Doris and Xanthippe.* This story consists of two separate episodes. The first episode centers on the four concubines of the prefect Agrippa and includes the functions of the apostle Peter arriving in town, the women going to hear him preach, the women vowing chastity, Agrippa attempting to violate their vows, the women resisting Agrippa, Agrippa imprisoning and attempting to kill Peter, and Peter dying. Four functions are omitted: the apostle encouraging the women (5), the women visiting the apostle in prison (8), and the women's persecution and rescue (11 and 12); also, the husband's defeat and women's freedom (13 and 14) are only implied, since the story does not explicitly state that the women continued in chastity after the apostle's death.

The second episode, centering on Xanthippe, wife of Albinus, almost exactly parallels the first. Functions 1, 2, 3, 4 and 6 are duplicated, whereas in 7, 9, and 10, the story of Xanthippe merges with that of the four concubines, when Albinus joins forces with Agrippa to kill Peter. Again, functions 13 and 14 are only implied.

(2) *The Story of Maximilla.* Maximilla's story contains all of the functions except persecution and rescue of the woman (11 and 12). However, function 2 is somewhat aberrant, in that the woman does not initially visit the apostle, but sends her friend to bring

him to her. Also, the apostle's healing of Maximilla, which follows, does not find a place in the typical sequence.

This healing story has parallels in a story found in the *Acts of John*,[7] in which Lycomedes seeks out the apostle John and asks him to heal his wife Cleopatra. Like Maximilla's husband Aegeates, Lycomedes threatens to kill himself if his wife dies. In both stories, the apostle rebukes the husband and heals the wife. In Maximilla's story, a healing story seems to have been incorporated into the typical chastity story. It is interesting to note that function 2 in the chastity story usually involves the woman's taking the initiative in approaching the apostle, whereas in the story of the healing of Cleopatra, it is the husband who initiates on behalf of the woman. Maximilla's story blends the two: as in Cleopatra's story, a third person must bring the apostle to the woman; but in the context of the chastity story, it is important that Maximilla herself requests that Andrew be brought to her, and she sends not her husband, but a female friend.

(3) *The Story of Drusiana.* Like the first story, this story should be divided into two separate episodes, the first involving Drusiana and Andronicus, the second Drusiana and Callimachus. The first episode, which is preserved only in secondary summaries and references seems to include all of the functions, except perhaps apostle encourages woman (5) and woman visits apostle in prison (8). It is not clear whether Andronicus attempts to kill the apostle John (functions 9 and 10) before, after, or at the same time that he persecutes his wife Drusiana by imprisoning her in a tomb (functions 11 and 12); if it occurs afterwards, it would seem to violate the sequence of the typical pattern. One other unusual aspect of the story is that the apostle's rescue (function 10) does not seem to involve the apostle's leaving the scene, as is the case in all other versions of the story type.

The second episode merges with the first in functions 1 through 3, while the remainder of the functions which appear are duplicated through the introduction of a second character in the role of "husband." Callimachus is not actually Drusiana's husband, but is a suitor who functions in the husband's role insofar as he threatens Drusiana's chastity. An interesting aspect of this particular episode is that the persecution of the woman (function 11) is not clearly distinct from the attempt to violate her vow (function 4). When Callimachus informs Drusiana of his sexual desire for her, she becomes ill and dies; thereafter, Callimachus attempts to violate her corpse. We seem justified in categorizing Drusiana's death as "persecution," since it so closely parallels her persecution in the first episode, where she is imprisoned inside a tomb as punishment for her refusal to have sexual relations with her husband Andronicus. Yet, in this second episode Drusiana's imprisonment in a tomb--that is, her death--is not explicitly presented as persecution (function 11) but rather as part of the attempted violation and resistance (functions 4 and 5). From Drusiana's point of view, Callimachus' sexuality is so horrifying that it literally kills her; yet even in death she cannot escape from the aggressive male threat, except through divine help. Callimachus finds Drusiana's resistance so frustrating that he would rather punish her, shame her, even kill her, than allow her to live freely, separate from him. The "husband's" persecution of the woman is thus an extension of his sexual aggression, and both arise at least partly out of his bewilderment and frustration at her defiance of his authority.

Still another significant aspect of this episode is the omission not only of functions 5 and 8--which, as is becoming clear, are omitted more often than not--but also of 7, 9, and 10: the imprisonment, attempted execution and death or rescue of the apostle.

(4) *The Story of Thecla.* Again, this story should be divided into two episodes. The Iconium episode includes all of the functions except that of the apostle encouraging the woman (function 5). Note that the "husband" role is filled in this first

episode by Thamyris, a fiance, and in the second by Alexander, a suitor.

In the Antioch episode, the first three functions merge with the first three functions of the first episode, but the other functions which appear are duplicated through the introduction of a second character in the "husband" role. In this episode function 5 is present in *inverse* form; that is, the apostle Paul not only fails to encourage the woman, but actually betrays her in a time of need:

> But immediately as they entered a Syrian by the name of Alexander, one of the first of the Antiochenes, seeing Thecla fell in love with her, and sought to win over Paul with money and gifts. But Paul said: "I do not know the woman of whom thou dost speak, nor is she mine."[8]

Related to this betrayal is the fact that functions 7, 9, and 10 (as well as 8) are omitted; in this episode, the apostle is not persecuted at all, but simply slips away unnoticed. Thecla, on the other hand, is dramatically persecuted in this second episode--as she was in the first.

The Thecla story also includes two segments which stand outside the two episodes and which do not find a place in the typical sequence of functions: Thecla's seeking and finding of Paul in chapters 23-25 and 40-43.

(5) *The Story of Artemilla and Eubula.* This story fits the story type least of all the chastity stories, and it is difficult to know how to judge its divergences, since it is preserved only in fragmentary form. The story as we have it begins with the apostle Paul already in prison. Artemilla's first visit to Paul (function 2) is identical with her visit to the apostle in prison (function 8) and includes a dramatic baptism account. No clear reference is made to Artemilla's decision to renounce sexual relations with her husband (function 3), though the jealousy of both her husband and the husband of her friend Eubula is mentioned, and this jealousy in-

cites both men to hurry Paul's execution. In other stories, these details are closely linked with the women's chastity, and perhaps they are in this case as well. Functions 7, 8, 9, 10, 13, and 14 are all included in the proper sequence, which might indicate that this is after all a typical chastity story which has been modified to fit into another story about Paul's imprisonment and near martyrdom.

(6) *The Story of the "Princess Bride."* The most unusual aspect of the story of the princess is that the father functions in the "husband" role, whereas the actual husband is so remarkably passive as to have almost no effect on the story at all. Consequently, the sexual aggression which usually accompanies the "husband's" attempt to violate the vow as well as his persecution of the apostle and the woman is toned down considerably. Also, though the king does attempt to imprison the apostle, he does not succeed in doing so. In one sense, this failure to imprison is not significantly different from the miraculous rescue of the apostle, which occurs in some other stories; however, the omission of the imprisonment and attempted execution does remove most of the conflict from the story. The battle is won almost too easily.

It seems likely that the author who put this story into literary form was more interested in presenting the success of the apostle's missionary activity than in telling a good story. Perhaps the author also wished to soften the more radical social implications of the story: note that it is the woman's father who summons the apostle, and that the woman is relatively easily reunited with the father. However, the *Acts of Thomas* also contains the story of Mygdonia and Tertia, which does not reflect this same conservatism.

(7) *The Story of Mygdonia and Tertia.* Once again, this is a story containing two distinct parallel episodes, which in this case are rather elaborately intertwined. The first episode, which centers around Mygdonia, contains all fourteen functions, some of which

appear in multiple cycles: the sequence of functions 2 through 6 is repeated three times before the story moves on to function 7.

The second episode, which centers on Tertia, merges at some points with Mygdonia's episode. Functions 1, 9, and 10 are the same for both, and functions 12, 13, and 14 occur simultaneously for both. This episode includes all the functions except function 5. In spite of its complexity, the story of Mygdonia and Tertia conforms remarkably closely to the typical pattern.

Table I at the end of this chapter summarizes the comparison of the eleven story-episodes with the proposed structural outline of the story type. The table confirms the basic structural similarities of the chastity stories. As was the case with Propp's Russian fairy tales, functions are sometimes omitted; and, as we have seen, roles are filled by different characters, and actions are carried out in different ways. However, the sequence of functions is followed in all cases. Only in the stories of Maximilla and Thecla does significant narrative material external to the type appear, and in both cases this seems to result from a merging of the chastity story with other story types; the case of Maximilla's healing with its parallel in the story of Cleopatra has already been mentioned, and parallels with the unusual material in the Thecla story will be discussed later in the chapter. We may conclude that the chastity stories all adhere to the structural type presented above, although each version differs significantly from the abstracted "type" as well as from the other versions.

Our review of the stories makes possible a more detailed definition of the structure. It appears that functions 5 and 8, both of which involve the apostle's encouragement of the woman, are optional; they are included in less than half of the stories. However, they are important for what they add to our understanding of the apostle's role. Functions 11 and 12, the persecution and rescue of the woman, are included more consistently but are omitted in five out of eleven episodes, or four out of seven stories.

Functions 7, 9, and 10, the imprisonment, persecution and death or rescue of the apostle, are omitted in two significant versions, both of which *do* include functions 11 and 12, persecution and rescue of the woman. Thus, persecution and rescue or death of either the woman or the apostle seems to be a necessary component of the story: all versions include either functions 7, 9, and 10 or functions 11 and 12, and some include both.

Analysis of the significance of these structural variations is aided by the use of the following terms borrowed from Propp's description of the functions of Russian fairy tales: preparatory section, villainy, struggle, victory, and lack liquidated.[9] The preparatory section of the chastity story, which includes functions 1 through 3, establishes the set of circumstances and relationships which will be placed in jeopardy in the course of the story. It also introduces the major character roles: the woman, the apostle, and the husband (the husband is usually introduced indirectly either in the identification of the woman as the "wife of X" or in the statement of her vow). "Villainy," function 4, is that act of the husband (the villain) which initiates the struggle between him and the woman (the heroine): the attempted violation of her vow. The struggle between the two results in the victory of the woman, which occurs in function 13. The husband may be converted (as in stories 3a, 3b, 5, and 6) and/or punished (as in stories 2, 3b, and 5), or he may simply be forced to recognize the ineffectiveness of his attempts to sway the woman. Following the woman's victory, in function 14, the initial lack or misfortune brought about by the act of villainy is removed: the woman is no longer threatened by her marital obligations, but is freed to live her life chastely.

This basic sequence of villainy, struggle, and victory, which occurs in functions 4, 6, and 13, is not particularly dramatic. The real drama of the story, the point at which the struggle defines itself in a series of vivid, decisive actions, occurs in secondary struggle-victory sequences of persecution and death or rescue. These secondary sequences are actually reflections of the struggle and victory of the basic sequence,[10] and they may continue to focus on the struggle between the woman and her husband, or they may shift to the struggle between apostle and husband; in the latter case, a second villainy function (imprisonment of the apostle) must be introduced to draw the apostle into the conflict. As we have seen, every story contains at least one secondary sequence; some contain both secondary sequences, but the focus tends to be on one or the other (as in 4a, where the focus is on the woman, and 7a and b, where the focus is on the apostle).

Table II at the end of this chapter presents the story structure in terms of its basic components of preparatory section, villainy, struggle, victory, and lack liquidated. The two alternative secondary sequences are distinguished from the basic sequence, and optional functions are bracketed.

In the chastity story structure as it is now defined, the woman fills the role of the heroine and the husband the role of the villain; the husband sometimes shares the villain's role with the governor, when those two characters are distinct. Only the role of the apostle remains to be clarified. In literary interpretations which emphasize not the structure of the story itself but rather the context of the story in the larger body of the apocryphal Acts, the apostle is often viewed as the hero of the story; the woman is thereby designated a passive role as victim, rather than heroine. A hero who acts on behalf of other victimized characters is known as a "seeker hero," and is contrasted with the "victimized hero," who acts on his or her own behalf.[11] Seeker heroes usually appear only when the victim is completely removed from the scene of action, as in a kidnapping. But the woman is neither entirely absent nor passive; and the major conflict with which the story begins and ends is the conflict between woman and husband, rather than apostle and husband. Not only is the struggle between husband and apostle omitted altogether in two versions of the story, but

even when it is emphasized, the apostle leaves the scene permanently in function 10, so that attention is shifted back to the
woman and husband for the conclusion of the story. It is therefore
difficult to identify the apostle as a seeker hero, the woman as a
victim; it is much more in harmony with the structure of the story
to view the woman as the victimized heroine.

What then is the role of the apostle in the chastity story, if
he is not the hero? In the second function, he is the one who gives
the woman the message of chastity. In the optional functions 5
and 8, he is the one who gives the woman strength and power to
endure in her struggle; sometimes this is transferred through his
words of encouragement, while in other versions, power is transferred concretely through the ritual of baptism (as in stories 5, 7a,
and 7b). In the majority of the stories, the apostle also serves as a
"proxy" for the woman in the secondary struggle-victory sequence
(functions 7, 9, and 10). In all these functions, the apostle bears
strong resemblance to the "donor" figure who is common to folktales.[12] Like the donor, the apostle gives the heroine something
which enables her to triumph in her struggle.

If the apostle, particularly in his "proxy" function, seems
to play a more active and prominent role than is typical for donor
figures, this too is significant. The very fact that the apostle is
sometimes mistakenly identified as the hero of the story reflects a
certain tension in the story, a competition between woman and
apostle for center stage. In one exceptional version of the chastity
story--the story of Xanthippe and the concubines--the last four
functions are omitted, so that the story ends with the focus having
shifted from the women to the apostle and his death. There are
many other martyrdom stories outside this collection in which the
conflict between martyr and governor is primary,[13] and the Xanthippe story may indicate that the chastity story has a tendency to
be merged with or transformed into a martyrdom story focusing on
the apostle. Particularly in their literary context as parts of the

Acts of the various apostles, pressure on the chastity stories to emphasize the role of the apostle is great. It is not surprising that the Xanthippe story has shifted somewhat away from the emphasis on the conflict between woman and husband; it is more significant that the other stories have not done so.

Comparison of the Chastity Story with the Novelistic Story

Two kinds of similarity between the chastity stories and the Hellenistic romantic novels are commonly noted: similarity of motifs and similarity of narrative structure. Motifs found in both the apocryphal Acts and the novel include: love at first sight, beautiful young women, frustrated lovers, journeys, changes of clothes, persecutions (abduction, sale into slavery, imprisonment, crucifixion, burning), miraculous rescue, visits in prison through bribery of the guard, emphasis on faithfulness, delaying tactics, oracles and prophetic dreams, etc. Such shared motifs do not in themselves indicate historical relationship between the stories. Motifs may be transmitted either literarily or orally (in fact, most of the motifs mentioned above are found in Thompson's *Motif-Index of Folk Literature*),[14] and they float easily from one story to another. The same motif may be found in many historically unrelated stories.

A common narrative structure may provide a stronger in-dication of historical relationship between stories, whether it be lit-erary or oral. Before considering the question of whether and/or how the chastity stories are related to the Hellenistic novel, it will be necessary to consider the narrative structure of the novels in order to clarify comparison of the two groups of stories.

Five major romantic novels have survived from the Hel-lenistic and Roman periods. Of the five, the two earliest are by Chariton and Xenophon of Ephesus; these pre-date the sophistic movement which began in the second century C.E. and produced the more refined novels of Longus, Achilles Tatius, and Heliodorus.

Chariton's *Chaereas and Callirhoe*[15] tells the story of two beautiful young Syracusans who fall deeply in love; the political rivalries of their families are overcome and they marry. But their happiness is brief, for Callirhoe's rejected suitors are resentful of Chaereas' success and seek revenge. The suitors trick Chaereas into believing falsely that Callirhoe has been unfaithful to him, and in his jealous passion Chaereas kicks Callirhoe, who falls to the ground as if dead. She is given a sumptuous burial, and when she regains consciousness, she finds herself in a tomb which is in the process of being robbed. The tomb robbers, shocked to realize that she is alive, decide to take her with them. They travel by ship to Ionia, where they sell her to a recently widowed nobleman named Dionysius. Dionysius falls in love with his beautiful slave. Callirhoe thinks only of Chaereas, but when she discovers she is pregnant with Chaereas' child, she agrees to marry Dionysius in order to insure a safe future for her child. She becomes renowned through all the land for her beauty, and a statue of her is placed in Aphrodite's shrine.

Meanwhile, Chaereas discovers the empty tomb and sets out to find out what has become of Callirhoe's body. He arrives in Ionia and sees Callirhoe's statue, but just as he is on the point of recovering her, he is overtaken by further misfortune. His ship is attacked and he is sold into slavery. At this point, the plot grows more complicated. Callirhoe's beauty has become so famous that noblemen and rulers from all over Asia Minor are scheming to steal her away from Dionysius; Chaereas is likewise trying to win her back. There is a trial, and a war, but finally Callirhoe and Chaereas are reunited and return to Syracuse.

The sequence of events in Xenophon's *Ephesian Tale*[16] is even more complex than in Chariton's novel. The basic framework of the story is as follows. The beautiful Habrocomes and Antheia fall in love. As the two begin to waste away with passion, their parents consult an oracle to discover the cause of their "disease." The oracle informs them of their children's love and predicts that Habrocomes and Antheia will marry, but will experience many sufferings at sea before attaining happiness. To satisfy the oracle, the parents arrange the marriage of their children and send them on a sea voyage. Habrocomes and Antheia are promptly captured by pirates and sold into slavery. Separated, they endure repeated persecutions and threats to their chastity, but they remain faithful and continue to search for one another. Like Callirhoe, Antheia is buried alive and kidnapped by tomb robbers. Also like Callirhoe, she is several times rescued from a desperate situation only to have her rescuer fall in love with her and attempt to seduce her. Once Antheia kills a robber with his own sword when he is on the point of violating her chastity. On another occasion, she is sold to a brothel owner and feigns epilepsy to escape her customers. Habrocomes likewise undergoes threats to his chastity: twice resentful women who have been unsuccessful in their efforts to seduce him accuse him falsely of attempting their own seduction. In one case, the false accusation involves a charge of murder as well, and Habrocomes is sentenced to both crucifixion and burning, but is miraculously saved on each occasion. Eventually, Habrocomes and Antheia are reunited and return to Ephesus where they live out their lives happily.

Longus' pastoral novel *Daphnis and Chloe*[17] unfolds at a much more subdued pace, and indeed resembles the other novels only in the most general outline of its story: a young couple fall in love and vow faithfulness; they undergo attempted seductions and kidnappings; eventually they are married and prosper. In this case, the two lovers are also foundlings, and at the end of the novel their true parents are discovered, which results in dramatic elevation of their social status.

In Achilles Tatius' *Clitophon and Leucippe*,[18] the young lovers flee from home after the heroine's mother discovers Clitophon in Leucippe's bed. In the course of their journey, they meet with the stock misfortunes: shipwreck, kidnapping by robbers and pirates, and sale into slavery, always accompanied by threats to chastity. The two are separated, and Clitophon thinks Leucippe dead. He marries the widow Melitte, but delays consummating the marriage out of respect for Leucippe's memory. Leucippe, who is not dead, becomes a slave on Melitte's estate. She initially feels reproach toward Clitophon because of his marriage, but she conceals her identity and learns that he has remained chaste. She reveals herself to Clitophon, but just when the two seem on the point of reunion, Melitte's first husband, thought dead, returns home. He imprisons Clitophon and atempts to seduce Leucippe, who resists him defiantly. Ironically, at this point Melitte sneaks into Clitophon's guarded room, and he finally submits to her sexual desires. He then dresses in her clothes and sneaks out, only to be captured again by the wronged husband. Eventually, the husband brings both Clitophon and Leucippe to trial on the charges of adultery and fleeing from a master respectively. In a dramatic trial, which involves a test of Leucippe's virginity, the lovers are freed and finally marry.

The last novel is Heliodorus' *Ethiopian Story*.[19] The heroine Charicleia is the daughter of the king and queen of Ethiopia, but is exposed as an infant and raised in Delphi, where she becomes a priestess of Artemis. She guards her chastity fiercely and has no interest in marrying until she meets the handsome Theagenes. The two elope and set out to find Charicleia's parents in Ethiopia; Charicleia insists that Theagenes swear to respect her chastity until their arrival in that country. As we might expect, that arrival comes none too soon: pirates, robbers, battles, sale into slavery, and many threats to chastity intervene. The two are separated, and Charicleia must search for Theagenes. Once reunited, they are cruelly tortured by a lecherous queen because of their insistence on chastity. She sentences Charicleia to be burned, but Charicleia is miraculously preserved. Eventually, the two are taken as prisoners of war by the king and queen of Ethiopia. Charicleia reveals to them that she is their daughter, and Charicleia and Theagenes are finally married.

These stories have less in common than do the chastity stories, and it is more difficult to view them as a single structural type. However, certain common features do emerge:

1. A young and beautiful couple fall in love and are betrothed or married.
2. They leave home on a ship voyage and become separated.
3. They endure persecutions and threats to their chastity, yet remain faithful.
4. They are reunited and return home.

To what extent do the chastity stories of the apocryphal Acts conform to this general structure? The first function appears only in a greatly modified form in the account of the meeting of the woman and the apostle, and in the woman's subsequent vow to chastity. There are indeed suggestions of repressed eroticism in the descriptions of the relationship of Thecla to Paul, of Maximilla to Andrew, or of Mygdonia to Thomas, for example, but the relationships of the women and the apostles are nevertheless not romantic relationships. Nor is faithfulness to the apostle ever explicitly mentioned; the woman's faithfulness is to Christ and God. Finally, the chastity stories differ from the novels in that it is always the woman who immediately "falls in love" with the apostle, while the apostle remains relatively passive. The novels, in contrast, always depict the experience of "love at first sight" as one which strikes both hero and heroine simultaneously.

The second novelistic function is absent in all of the chastity stories but one. Only the Thecla story contains any journey or separation. When the apostle leaves or dies in the other chastity stories, it is not problematic, nor does it represent an obstacle to be overcome. In the third function, the chastity stories again differ from most of the novels in that the experience of threatened chastity is not mutual but affects only the women; also, the persecutions suffered by the apostles and, less frequently, by the women in the stories do not include shipwreck, kidnapping, and sale into slavery,[20] the most common persecutions in the novel, but center on the political persecution. Finally, the fourth function is again greatly modified in the chastity stories: the woman and the apostles are "reunited" only in the sense that the woman reaches a point of sureness and security in her chastity which unites her "spiritually" with the apostle and his message.

Given all of these differences, and particularly the absence of the function involving the journey and problematic separation in all of the chastity stories except Thecla's story, it does not seem likely that the basic novelistic structure of the love story served as the primary source or shaper of the narrative structure of the chastity stories.

Common Tale Types Underlying the Novel and the Thecla Story

Though the basic narrative structure of the novel is quite different from that of the typical chastity story, the novelistic stories about chastity and faithfulness do appear to be related both to the Thecla story and to a number of folktales whose "types" are described in the tale type index compiled by Antti Aarne and Stith Thompson.[21] "Tale type" here refers not to a structurally defined type, but to a description of a group of folk-stories which are assumed to be historically related; variants of a single structural type may or may not be historically related, while variants of a single tale type always are.

Chariton's novel offers the clearest evidence of folk derivation. Compare his story with the following tale type description:

A merchant's son marries the king's daughter. An attempt is made to seduce her. The man strikes his wife and thinks he has killed her. A physician heals her and wants to secure her for himself. She flees in men's clothes. Becomes emperor. Has her picture displayed in a public place. Is reunited with her husband. (AT 881)[22]

The parallels are very close. Callirhoe is the daughter of the first citizen of Syracuse, whereas Chaereas' social status is somewhat lower. The suitors pretend to seduce Callirhoe. In his jealousy, Chaereas strikes her and thinks he has killed her. While no physician heals Callirhoe, she is on several occasions rescued by men who then try to "secure her for themselves." She does not become emperor, but does become the famous wife of a nobleman and has her statue displayed in a public place. Chariton's novel appears to be based on the variant of a common folktale.

An important aspect of Chariton's story is that it is the husband's doubt and betrayal which make it necessary for the innocent woman to leave home and expose herself to the further persecution of "physician-villains." This element of betrayal is also present in the last section of Achilles Tatius' novel, in which Clitophon marries another woman and Leucippe becomes a slave on his new wife's estate. With hair cropped, she is not recognized, and she conceals her identity until she learns of Clitophon's faithfulness. While the parallels are not as close as is the case with Chariton's story, this story may be compared with the following two tale types:

A prince forsakes his fiancee in order to pledge himself to another of his father's choice. In men's clothes, the first fiancee along with her companions goes into the service of the prince. Test: whether men or maidens. The prince marries his first fiancee. (AT 884)[23]

I. A princess is alone in a tower or gorgeous tent. A prince finds her and they fall in love, but he leaves or the princess's father offers his daughter in marriage to the prince, who refuses. II. (a) She pursues the prince disguised as a man, succeeds eventually in being recognized as he is about to marry another; or (b) She pursues in a ship, builds a palace opposite the prince and is eventually recognized; or (c) She pursues and as servant-maid wins the prince's love. (AT 891A)[24]

In both of these tale types, as in Achilles Tatius' novel, the hero betrays his fiancee, and she must travel after him and become a slave in order to win him back.

But the lover's or husband's betrayal is not the only force which sends heroines on journeys, and indeed is not a favored theme of the novelists, who are interested in portraying both hero and heroine in the best possible light. Achilles Tatius offers a different explanation for his heroine's initial flight from her family and home: the threat of persecution from her parents because of her suspected relations with Clitophon. Heliodorus uses a similar device to explain Charicleia's flight from home: she must elude her father's plans to marry her to a man she doesn't love. In both novels, the heroine flees with her lover but becomes separated and exposed to the threats of pirates, robbers, and other lechers. While it is difficult to identify these stories with any single tale type in the tale type index, they do share certain features in common with the body of folktales which describe a "double persecution of the heroine, both in her parental home and in her husband's house."[25] The first anticipated persecution of both Leucippe and Charicleia is from parents, while the second set of persecutions occurs under the supposed protection of the husband's presence.

In Longus' novel--which is the most unique of the novels-- the journey and persecutions do not play as large a role as they do in the other novels and folktales. Xenophon's novel, on the other hand, is quite typical, but is also notably confused in its narrative structure. Reardon wittily describes the "dire literary straits" into which Xenophon is led, primarily due to his "lacking a mainspring for his story."[26]   Comparing Xenophon's novel to Chariton's, Reardon notes,

> Chariton used the marriage also to launch his story; it is
> Chaereas' jealousy that leads to the abduction of Cal-
> lirhoe. But Xenophon is in this respect quite singularly
> inept. The oracle which he invents in order to keep the
> idea of divine providence before the reader not only does
> not give impetus to the plot, it actually hamstrings its
> development; it is only in *defiance* of its predictions that
> the young couple's parents send their children abroad.
> Having predicted difficulties for Habrocomes and An-
> theia, the gods keep their word. Hero and heroine wan-
> der all over the Mediterranean world, Asia, Egypt, Sicily,
> but for no very good reasons; at each move they could as
> well go somewhere else, or indeed stay where they are;
> no logic, no necessity guides their steps. Xenophon can-
> not count on the structure of his story to sustain interest
> (as Chariton can), and falls back on melodrama and
> bizarre incident.[27]

Xenophon's novel represents in extreme form a tendency which is present in all the novels. The stories which provide the overall logic of the narrative, which shape the elements of journey, perse- cution, and marriage into a meaningful whole, are increasingly ig- nored in favor of greater emphasis on the description of isolation and persecution experienced by the hero and heroine. The ten- sions between man and woman or parent and child inherent in the original folktales which appear to have given the novels their basic shape are deemphasized; instead, the novels focus on the common experience of insecurity and the common hope for the security of human love or divine salvation. Interestingly, stories which traditionally describe the persecution suffered by women seem in the literary context of the Hellenistic novel to be modified to apply to men as well.[28]

While the narratives which provide the overarching structure of the novel may become blurred or even be discarded, as in the case of Xenophon's novel, the shorter story units describing the various persecutions of heroine or hero are more successful in retaining their narrative shape and logic and can be identified with even greater certainty as folk-stories. Xenophon's novel is particularly packed with such stories. His hero Habrocomes is twice unjustly accused of seduction, in narratives conforming to a story type which is well known in the versions of Joseph and Potiphar's wife, Hippolytus and Phaedra, and Susanna and the Elders. The stories of Antheia's slaying the robber and evading suitors in the brothel have parallels in one of the elder Seneca's controversy stories, as well as in later Christian and Jewish stories.[29] These stories do not directly involve either the journey or the relationship of hero and heroine, but focus more narrowly on the theme of threatened chastity.

A number of different folk-stories thus underlie the novels, both in their overarching framework and in their individual incidents. Interestingly, several of these stories appear to be related to the Thecla story as well as to the novels. We have seen that her story shares the characteristic novelistic elements of journey and problematic separation of the "lovers"; those elements, in addition to the element of the apostle's betrayal, distinguish the Thecla story from the other versions of the chastity story and suggest its possible identification with other folktales.[30]

The first episode of the Thecla story can be described in terms of the typical chastity story sequence of functions; it omits only the optional function 5. (1) Paul arrives in town. (2) Thecla hears Paul preach and (3) vows chastity. (4) Her fiance Thamyris attempts to violate that vow, and (6) Thecla resists his attempt. (7) Thamyris incites the governor to imprison Paul. (8) Thecla visits Paul in prison. (9) The governor sentences Paul to be scourged and (10) driven out of town. (Note that Paul neither dies nor is miraculously rescued, but exits on a less triumphant note). (11) Thecla is sentenced to be burned to death. She looks around for Paul "as a lamb in the wilderness looks about for the shepherd,"[31] but he is not there; instead, Christ appears to her in the form of Paul to give her strength. (12) Rain and hail miraculously quench the fire, and (13-14) Thecla goes free.

Next comes a section which does not fit the typical structure. Thecla searches for Paul and finds him outside the city.

> And Thecla said to Paul: "I will cut my hair short and follow thee wherever thou goest." But he said: "The season is unfavourable, and thou art comely. May no other temptation come upon thee, worse than the first, and thou endure not and play the coward!" And Thecla said: "Only give me the seal in Christ, and temptation shall not touch me." And Paul said: "Have patience, Thecla, and thou shalt receive the water."[32]

As in function 11 above, Paul fails to give Thecla the encouragement and empowering which she requests, and which apostle-donors usually give.

The second episode, which follows this section, skips over the preparatory section already established in the first episode and begins with function 4. (4) Alexander falls in love with Thecla and tries to buy her from Paul. (5) At this point, Paul not only fails to support Thecla, but actively betrays her: "But Paul said, 'I do not know the woman of whom thou dost speak, nor is she mine.'"[33] Alexander presses still further in his "villainy" and embraces Thecla on the street. As in the first episode, Thecla "looks about

for Paul" in vain.[34]   (6) Left to her own resources, she resists
Alexander violently, ripping his cloak and tearing the crown from
his head. Paul seems to have disappeared from the scene, and
functions 7-10 (persecution of the apostle) are omitted. (11) Thecla
is sentenced to the wild beasts. (12) In the course of a dramatic
fight, she baptizes herself and is miraculously saved four times.
(13) The governor is forced to discontinue the execution and (14)
lets her go free.

The final section is not part of the typical sequence. After
being released, Thecla stays and teaches and converts a number of
women to Christianity. But she yearns for Paul, so she dresses as
a man, takes with her a retinue of followers, and goes off in search
of the apostle. When she finds him, he is astonished at the sight of
her and wonders "whether another temptation was not upon
her."[35] Thecla tells him all that has happened, and Paul is reas-
sured. Thecla then declares her intention to return to preach in
Iconium, her hometown, and Paul finally gives his blessing in the
form of a commission: "Go and teach the word of God!"[36] Thecla
does so.

Both the variations in the typical episodes and the inclu-
sion of the connecting narratives serve to give the story a distinctive twist. Unlike the apostle in the other stories, Paul is portrayed
as one who doubts and abandons the woman. In order to gain
Paul's approval, Thecla must prove her trustworthiness; she must
also travel in search of Paul and does so dressed in men's clothes.

These distinctive aspects of Thecla's story link it with the
following tale types listed in the tale type index, two of which also
possess close similarities to the novelistic stories:

A merchant's son marries the king's daughter. An attempt is made to seduce her. The man strikes his wife
and thinks he has killed her. A physician heals her and
wants to secure her for himself. She flees in men's

clothes. Becomes emperor. Has her picture displayed in a public place. Is reunited with her husband. (AT 881)[37]

A ship captain marries a poor girl. Makes a wager with a merchant on the chastity of his wife. Through treachery, the merchant secures a token of unfaithfulness (ring). The captain leaves home. The wife follows him in men's clothing. They reach home again and everything is explained. (AT 882)[38]

I. A princess is alone in a tower or gorgeous tent. A prince finds her and they fall in love, but he leaves or the princess's father offers his daughter in marriage to the prince, who refuses. II. (a) She pursues the prince disguised as a man, succeeds eventually in being recognized as he is about to marry another; or (b) She pursues in a ship, builds a palace opposite the prince and is eventually recognized; or (c) She pursues and as servant-maid wins the prince's love. (AT 891A)[39]

While the Thecla story is not identical with any of these tale types, the parallels are striking. Like type 881, the Thecla story begins with a "marriage" (Thecla's vow to Christ/Paul) and attempted seduction. Paul does not strike Thecla and think that he has killed her, but he does doubt her faithfulness and twice abandons her to a probable death. Christ, who is commonly referred to as "Physician" in the apocryphal Acts, saves Thecla from death; he does not, however, subsequently attempt to retain her or seduce her, as in the tale type. Thecla, like the woman in the folktale, dresses in men's clothes. She does not become emperor, but does receive baptism and becomes a Christian teacher. She also does not have her picture displayed, but instead appears rather dramatically in person to Paul. As in the folktale--but unlike the typical chastity story--the two are reunited in the end. Tale types 882 and 891A also both share with the Thecla story the basic sequence of marriage or love, abandonment (and in 882, this is in consequence of the man's doubts about the woman's chastity), the woman's pursuit of the husband or lover in men's clothing, and the final reunion.

Precisely those elements which distinguish the Thecla story from the other versions of the chastity type are found in these common folktales. The probability that the Thecla story is historically related to oral versions of these folktales is strengthened by the fact that two of these folktales have more direct parallels in the contemporary novels of Chariton and Achilles Tatius. The elements shared by the Thecla story and the Hellenistic novels could very likely be based on related oral sources. That neither the author of the *Acts of Paul* nor Chariton nor Achilles Tatius "invented" the basic shape of the story is evidenced by the parallels listed in the tale type index; moreover, the striking differences between their versions makes direct literary borrowing between them seem unlikely.

Summary and Conclusions

Structural analysis of the seven "chastity stories" found in the apocryphal Acts has proven that these stories do indeed conform to a common "type." The closeness of the similarities between the stories suggests that they are all historically related to one another. More literary critical work remains to be done on the apocryphal Acts in order to establish to what degree the five earliest Acts are literarily dependent on one another.[40] However, the chastity stories themselves do not betray clear signs of literary dependence, and the significant variations among them indicate a greater likelihood that the variant versions of the legend originated in oral tradition before being put in literary form. The fact that the chastity story shifts from one setting and group of characters to another without in any way qualifying its claim to be a true, historical account further strengthens the theory that the stories are the products of oral tradition, not the conscious creations of authors.

Some versions of the chastity story appear to consist of a "merging" of a typical chastity story with another folk narrative. The story of Maximilla is combined with a healing story, and all of the chastity stories are combined to some degree with a martyrdom story; it is difficult at this point to ascertain whether the chastity story ever existed independently of the martyrdom story, since it is unlikely that such independent versions would have survived. Finally, the most striking example of a "merging" is the Thecla story, which appears to be strongly influenced by folktales in which a heroine is abandoned by a hero whom she must pursue in men's clothing in order to win him back.

This folktale influence links the Thecla story to those versions of the novelistic story in which the elements of abandonment and pursuit are also present. Indeed, the novels appear to be even more closely related to known folktales than is the Thecla story. In the case of the novel, folklore origin for much of the narrative structure can be demonstrated conclusively. Common oral sources for the Thecla story and the novels provide the most likely explanation for their similarities. The other chastity stories are not directly related to the stories of the novel, though they do share a focus on the threat and victorious defense of chastity. This focus can be found in many other stories of the same period as well (for example, the various versions of chastity defended in a brothel and of the Hippolytus-Phaedra story) and does not indicate that one set of stories directly influenced the other, much less that the literary version of the novel shaped the stories of the apocryphal Acts.

The clear differences between the chastity stories of the apocryphal Acts and the romantic novels have important implications not only for an understanding of origins but for an understanding of meaning as well. All too often in the past an eagerness to identify the chastity stories as novels has led scholars to over-look their uniqueness and to romanticize their message.

The most striking difference between the Christian story and the novel is in their attitudes toward society. Reardon describes the novel as "personal myth," which he contrasts with the "social myth" of New Comedy and the "political myth" of epic and tragedy, and he describes the cultural conditions of the imperial age which gave rise to the personal orientation of the novel.[41] The heroine and hero of the novel, like many women and men of their age, feel themselves to be isolated and even alienated from the world around them; they are lonely journeyers on an alien sea, and the happiness they seek is in their personal relationship to a lover or a god. Reardon notes that the novel's heroine and hero share their search for a personal salvation with religious enthusiasts of their day, and he remarks that the readers of the novel "formed the layer of population in which the salvationist religions made such headway."[42]

Though the personal focus of the novel cannot be denied, the novel also takes the social conventions of its time for granted. Heroine and hero undertake a journey during which they are iso-lated and alienated from the society around them; however, the happiness for which they strive and which they attain in the end is social as well as personal. Marriage and family are affirmed in the novel, and the broader community of city or town is also present in positive aspect. Hero and heroine may find themselves isolated, but they strive to return home to their families and communities and above all to each other.

The Christian chastity story, on the other hand, is not merely apolitical and asocial, as Reardon describes the novel, but is explicitly *opposed* to the political and social orders, above all to marriage and family. Whereas the novel begins with mutual love and ends with marriage and reunion with family, the chastity story begins with the woman's attraction to the apostle and his message and ends with the woman's triumphant attainment of singleness. The heroine and hero of the novel leave home and discover persecution; the woman of the chastity story does not journey but experiences alienation in her own family and community. Whereas the novel attempts to portray chastity as a virtue of both women and men, and a virtue which serves to strengthen the bond between women and men, the Christian chastity story focuses only on the woman; even when the apostle is persecuted, it is not on account of his own chastity but on account of the woman's chastity, and the woman's chastity destroys rather than strengthens her relationships with most men.[43]   In their attitude toward the society around them, the novel and the Christian chastity story thus take extremely different stances, and chastity in particular has a dramatically different social significance in the two groups of stories.

The chastity stories are not fictional tales of romantic love between a man and a woman; they are legends, claiming to present the "true story" of the radical alienation of a woman from her society. Von Dobschütz' theory has proved misleading: the chastity stories must be interpreted in their own right, not simply reduced to "Christian novels."

TABLE

I

FUNCTION	Concubines 1a	Xanthippe 1b	Maximilla 2	Drusiana 1 3a	Drusiana 2 3b	Thecla 1 4a	Thecla 2 4b	Artemilla 5	Princess 6	Mygdonia 7a	Tertia 7b
1 A arrives	X	X	X	X	←	X	←	(X)	X	X	←
2 W goes to A	X	X	V	X	←	X	←	?	V	X	X
3 W vows chastity	X	X	X	X	←	X	←	?	X	X	X
4 H violates vow	X	X	X	X	X	X	X		X	X	(X)
5 A encourages W			X				--		X		
6 W resists H	X	X	X	X	X	X	X		X	X	(X)
7 H imprisons A	X	←	X	X		X		X	--	X	X
8 W visits A			X			X		V		X	X
9 H kills A	X	←	X	X		X		X		X	←
10 A dies/rescued	X	←	X	V		X		X	X	X	←
11 H persecutes W				X	X	X	X			X	X
12 W is rescued				X	X	X	X			X	X
13 W defeats H	(X)	(X)	X	X	X	X	X	X	X	X	X
14 W is freed	(X)	(X)	X	X	X	X	X	X	X	X	X

X   :   function appears in story

←   :   function appears, but is merged with same function in paired episode

V   :   function appears in unusual form

--   :   function appears in inverse form

(X) :   function is implied but not explicitly stated

TABLE II

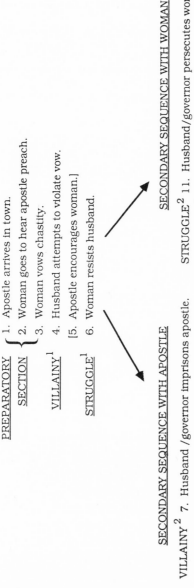

PREPARATORY SECTION { 1. Apostle arrives in town.
2. Woman goes to hear apostle preach.
3. Woman vows chastity.

VILLAINY^1 4. Husband attempts to violate vow.

[5. Apostle encourages woman.]

STRUGGLE^1 6. Woman resists husband.

SECONDARY SEQUENCE WITH WOMAN

STRUGGLE^2 11. Husband/governor persecutes woman.

VICTORY^2 12. Woman is rescued.

SECONDARY SEQUENCE WITH APOSTLE

VILLAINY^2 7. Husband/governor imprisons apostle.

[8. Woman visits apostle in prison.]

STRUGGLE^2 9. Husband/governor attempts to kill apostle.

VICTORY^2 10. Apostle dies or is rescued.

VICTORY^1 13. Woman defeats husband/governor.

LACK LIQUIDATED 14. Woman is free.

Notes

1 Stith Thompson, *Motif-Index of Folk Literature* (Indiana Univ. Press, 1957). Though Thompson's index was not yet available when Rosa Söder did her work, she used motifs as the basis of her argument for the identity of the apocryphal Acts as folkstories; see pp. 16-19 above. Dennis MacDonald followed Alex Olrick, "Epic Laws of Folk Narrative," in identifying the folkloristic character of the *Acts of Paul* on the basis of narrative technique; see pp. 22-23 above.

2 Vladimir Propp, *Morphology of the Folktale*, 2nd ed. (Austin: Univ. of Texas Press, 1968), p. 15.

3 Ibid., p. 11.

4 Ibid., p. 114.

5 See Lord Raglan, *The Hero: A Study in Tradition, Myth and Drama* (NY: Vintage, 1956); Raglan applies a "Proppian" approach to the analysis of hero legends.

6 See Appendix for summaries of each of the stories and for references to their translations in Hennecke.

7 *Acts of John*, Hennecke, *New Testament Apocrypha*, pp. 216-20.

8 *Acts of Paul*, ibid., p. 360.

9 Propp, pp. 25-65. The applicability of these terms, which were derived from Russian fairy tales, to the chastity stories as well as to many other tales suggests that the broad structural pattern described by these terms is favored by Indo-European folk narratives.

10 See especially the discussion of Drusiana and Callimachus, pp. 36-37 above.

11 Propp, p. 36.

12 Propp, pp. 39-50, 79.

13 See *The Acts of the Christian Martyrs*, ed. H. Musurillo (Oxford: Clarendon Press, 1972) for a collection of early Christian martyrdom accounts.

14 See especially types T15, T75, K1836, K1837, R12, R40-50, R61, R100-191, T32.1, and K1227.

[15] Chariton, *Chaereas and Callirhoe*, trans. W. E. Blake (Ann Arbor: Univ. of Michigan Press, 1939).

[16] Xenophon, *An Ephesian Tale*, in *Three Greek Romances*, trans. Moses Hadas (Indianapolis, NY & Kansas City: Bobbs-Merrill Co., Inc., 1953).

[17] Longus, *Daphnis and Chloe*, in *Three Greek Romances*, trans. Moses Hadas (Indianapolis, NY & Kansas City: Bobbs-Merrill Co., Inc., 1953).

[18] Achilles Tatius, *Clitophon and Leucippe*, trans. S. Gaselee, Loeb Classical Library (NY: G. P. Putnam's Sons, 1917).

[19] Heliodorus, *Ethiopian Story*, trans. W. Lamb (NY: E. P. Dutton & Co., 1961).

[20] Shipwreck occurs in the *Acts of Peter* and sale into slavery in the *Acts of Thomas*, but neither of these is connected with the chastity story.

[21] Antti Aarne, Stith Thompson, *The Types of the Folktale* (Helsinkii Academia Scientiarum Fennica, 1961). This index includes descriptions of tale types and lists examples of each type; it includes stories from Europe and the Americas, as well as some Asian tales.

[22] Ibid., p. 298.

[23] Ibid., p. 301.

[24] Ibid., p. 306.

[25] Ilana Dan, "The Innocent Persecuted Heroine: An Atttempt at a Model for the Surface Level of the Narrative Structure of the Female Fairy Tale," *Patterns in Oral Literature*, ed. Jason and Segal (The Hague, Paris: Mouton publishers, 1977), p. 13. See also Ilse Nolting-Hauff, "Märchenromane mit leidenden Helden," *Poetica* 6 (1974):417-55. Nolting-Hauff develops the structural parallels between the Hellenistic romantic novels and the general category of "fairy tales with victimized heroes." She does not focus on the role of women in these tales, but does note that aside from brother-sister pairs, there are few victimized *couples* in fairy tales: "usually only the bride is victimized" (p. 422).

[26] Reardon, "The Greek Novel," p. 298.

[27] Ibid., p. 299.

28 Even the novels, however, tend to portray the women as suffering more, particularly as regards threatened chastity. In Chariton's novel, Callirhoe suffers persecution almost from the beginning, when Chaereas kicks her in the stomach; when Chaereas suffers later as a slave, it is briefer and more deserved, and never includes threats to his chastity. In Achilles Tatius' novel, the heroine complains to the hero: "You know what I have suffered for your sake, but perforce I must remind you of it.... And was this all that I might become to another man what you have become to another woman? Never. I, through all these trials, have persevered to the end; you were never sold, never scourged, but you are marrying" (V.18, p. 277). Finally, Heliodorus' novel, though it includes abundant suffering for hero as well as heroine, clearly focuses interest more on Charicleia, her sufferings, her search for Theagenes, and her initiative in getting both herself and him out of desperate situations.

29 Seneca tells a story about a virgin priestess who was captured by pirates and sold into prostitution; she succeeded in preserving her chastity, and on one occasion killed a man with his own sword when he tried to force himself on her (*Controversia* I.2). Christian versions of the story include the story of Irene in the *Martyrdom of Agape, Irene and Chione*; the story of Trophima in the *Liber de Miraculis Beati Andreae Apostoli*; and the story of the virgin in Ambrose's *De Virginibus* II.4.22. Still another version appears in the Babylonian Talmud, *Abodah Zarah* I.17b-18b.

30 See pp. 37-38 above.

31 *Acts of Paul*, Hennecke, p. 358.

32 *Acts of Paul*, ibid., p. 360.

33 *Acts of Paul*, ibid.

34 *Acts of Paul*, ibid.

35 *Acts of Paul*, ibid., p. 364.

36 *Acts of Paul*, ibid.

37 Aarne-Thompson, p. 298.

38 Ibid., p. 299.

39 Ibid., p. 306.

40 Where literary dependence of one of the Acts upon another can be demonstrated, the possibility that at least some versions of the chastity story may be literarily dependent on one another must

be considered. C. Schmidt, "Zur Datierung der alten Petrusakten," *Zeitschrift für die neutestamentliche Wissenschaft und die Kunde der älteren Kirche* 29 (1930):150-55, maintains that the author of the *Acts of Paul* was familiar with the *Acts of Peter*. Other cases of dependence have been suggested, but up to the present none has been persuasively argued.

[41] Reardon, pp. 292-94.

[42] Ibid., p. 296.

[43] In her comparison of the *Life of Melania the Younger* and the Hellenistic novels, Elizabeth Clark eloquently describes the differences in their treatments of chastity: "In truth, the difference in sexual tone between the novels and early Christian literature is extreme. In the novels, if the couple remains chaste throughout, it is so that the nuptial chamber will figure more prominently at the story's end. The hero and heroine lust after each other and avoid sexual relationship only through considerable self-restraint. In some cases, their abstinence is not even intentional: indeed, Leucippe and Clitophon are already bedded down when Leucippe's mother interrupts their sexual initiation (she has had a portending dream regarding a robber with a naked sword). In *Daphnis and Chloe*, the young shepherd and shepherdess initially remain chaste simply because they do not understand how to perform the sexual act, despite close observation of their flocks. The difference here between the novels and Christian literature calls to mind Clement of Alexandria's observation that pagan sexual morality aimed merely at the control of sexual desire, whereas Christian teaching advocated the extirpation of desire itself. Such indeed is the gap in sentiment between the novels and early Christian literature." *The Life of Melania the Younger* (NY & Toronto: The Edwin Mellen Press, 1984), p. 163.

III. THE CHASTITY STORIES' TELLERS

At the end of the second century Tertullian wrote complaining of some Christians who called upon the example of Thecla "in support of women's right to teach and baptize" (*De Bapt.* I.17). This brief reference is our only shred of direct evidence concerning the tellers and audiences of the chastity stories. Who were the people who told the Thecla story? Were they women? Were they ascetics? Did they know the story from oral tradition or from the written version in the *Acts of Paul*? Did they know other versions of the chastity story? Neither Tertullian nor any other ancient writer gives a clear answer to these questions.

Determining the date and location of the apocryphal Acts is extremely difficult. Four of the five were probably compiled in the second half of the second century; the *Acts of Thomas* appears to have been written in the early third century. The *Acts of Peter, Paul* and *John* are likely to have originated in Asia Minor, the *Acts of Thomas* in Syria, and the *Acts of Andrew* in either Asia or Greece. We can surmise that the chastity stories circulated during the mid-second century--and perhaps earlier as well[1]--among the Hellenistic communities of the eastern Mediterranean.

While direct evidence concerning the tellers and audiences may be lacking, there are indirect indications that the chastity stories were told primarily by and to women. First, there is cross-cultural evidence, including evidence from Greco-Roman culture, which suggests that women in the second-century Hellenistic communities where the chastity stories originated would have produced and transmitted distinct bodies of women's stories. Second, the chastity stories seem to present a woman's point of view.

Women in Community: Story-Tellers

Hellenistic society upheld the ideal of a strict spatial and functional separation of males and females; whereas the public sphere was the domain of men, women were located in the private sphere:

> Marketplaces and council-halls and law-courts and gatherings and meetings where a large number of people are assembled, and open-air life with full scope for discussion and action--all these are suitable to men both in war and peace. Women are best suited to the indoor life which never strays from the house. (Philo, *The Special Laws*, III.169)

Typically, societies which enforce such separation of spheres produce significant bodies of "sex-specific" folklore:

> Women are excluded from some of men's expressive events and men are prohibited from some of women's expressive activities. In Iraq a man's presence is enough to terminate a miming event among women. In Morocco men are ignorant of a body of women's folklore that comes into play only when women are together.[2]

A folklorist describes story-telling among Near Eastern Jews similarly:

> We see a great diversity in story-telling habits. With our narrators' reminiscences we can distinguish here between story-telling sessions . . . which have a male and those which have a female audience, and others with a

sexually mixed audience. The same tales are not for every audience.[3]

Not only are there distinct bodies of women's stories, but there are also typical settings for the telling of women's stories:

> Men's activities usually take place in public arenas, women's in more private ones . . . . Thus, Hannerz found men talking on street corners and Bauman found them talking in a general store, whereas Fernea found women talking behind walls and closed doors. Stoeltje found women's talk performances in homes among friends. Claudia Mitchell-Kernan found female correlates to men's speech (long recognized as performance) both in the home and in mixed-group interaction outside the home.[4]

Among Near Eastern Jews,

> The male reconteur will perform before a larger audience; the female, more in the family circle and to an audience of other females.[5]

Likewise, Bertha, a typical woman storyteller from Pennsylvania, "tells her personal experience narratives not in public, like Elmer, but very much in private."

> In the private sphere, with its atmosphere of intimacy, Bertha and her women relatives thrive. When they feel close and comfortable with one another, when they perceive that everyone will listen and talk, their storytelling begins. This sphere of theirs may be indoors or outdoors, in any room or on any lawn; the location does not matter to their storytelling as much as the privacy that those locations afford.[6]

Because of the "private" location of women's story-telling, history, which has been shaped primarily by the events and activities of the public sphere, contains but meager evidence of Hellenistic women's folklore. We do, however, know that Greco-

Roman women were avid storytellers. As early as the seventh century B.C.E., Semonides witnesses to the Greek women's habit of sitting together to "tell stories about love" (*On Women* 83-93). The novelist Achilles Tatius, a closer contemporary of the chastity storytellers, remarks, "The race of women loves stories."[7] Contemporary Christian writers in Alexandria also refer to women's love of story-telling:

> Storytellers spend the whole day with the women, idly spinning erotic legends . . . . (Clement of Alexandria, *Paed.* 3.4)

> Would not an old woman who sings a story to lull a little child to sleep have been ashamed to whisper such tales as these . . . ? (Origen, *C. Celsum* 6.34)

Dennis MacDonald has collected further references to women's story-telling activity in the ancient world; these span the years from classical Greece to imperial Rome:

> Then we must first of all, it seems, control the story-tellers. Whatever noble story they compose we shall select, but a bad one we must reject. Then we shall persuade nurses and mothers to tell their children those we have selected and by those stories to fashion their minds far more than they can shape their bodies by handling them. The majority of the stories they now tell must be thrown out. (Plato, *Republic* II, 377c).

> Possibly, however, you regard this as an old wives' tale, and despise it. (Plato, *Gorgias* 527A).

> Now let me tell you some old women's tales to make you feel a little better. (Apuleius, *The Golden Ass*, 4,28).[8]

> Your stories still remain old wives' tales. (Lucian, *The Lover of Lies* 9).

> Poetry is a fable-prating old woman, who has been permitted to invent . . . whatever she deems suitable for

purposes of entertainment. (Eratosthenes, as para-
phrased by Strabo, *Geography* 1,2,3,C16).

For in dealing with a crowd of women . . . a philosopher
cannot influence them by reason or exhort them to rever-
ence, piety and faith; no, there is need of superstitious
fear also, and this is not possible without mythic tales
and miracles. (Strabo, *Geography* 1,2,3,C19).

Avoid the profane tales told by old women. (*1 Timothy*
4.7).

As MacDonald notes, most of these references to women's tale-
telling are disparaging, and several seek to limit the story-telling
activity. The disparaging descriptions of women's stories should
not, however, lead to the inference that the stories told by women
were necessarily insignificant, silly, or uninteresting; what these
descriptions do indicate is that the women's stories were viewed by
their society as "nonlegitimate genres," much as they are in our
own culture.

Female expressive forms either fit the male mold or they
are relegated to a nonlegitimate, less-than-expressive
category. For instance, we have "tall tales," a male genre
of story-telling; the female corollary is exaggeration. Men
have "stories" or "yarns"; women "gossip" or
"clothesline."[9]

As is the case with most "nonlegitimate" activities, women's story-
telling seems to have appeared threatening to those male authors
who attempted to silence the stories. Aristophanes' plays provide
early evidence that at least some Greek men feared that women's
gathering and story-telling might lead to their rebelliousness.[10]

These references to women's story-telling in Greco-Roman
society suggest the high likelihood that the women of the Hellenistic communities of the eastern Mediterranean would have produced and transmitted "sex-specific" women's folk-stories. This
claim is supported by the chastity stories themselves, which de-

scribe a world in which women spend most of their time with other women in the "private sphere" and share news and stories with one another.[11]

In the first chastity story, Agrippina, Nicaria, Euphemia and Doris go together to hear Peter and agree "with each other"[12] to renounce intercourse with Agrippa; they also share the news of their conversion with Xanthippe, who subsequently accompanies them to visit Peter and decides to separate from her husband as well. In another story, Thecla, though a stranger in the city of Antioch, immediately finds an enthusiastically supportive community of women there who attempt to intercede on her behalf when she is sentenced to the beasts and who aid her in escaping from the beasts; Thecla becomes particularly intimate with the widow Tryphaena and the women of her household, with whom she shares the Christian teachings. Artemilla likewise has a close female friend, Eubula, who tells her about Paul's message and accompanies her to visit the apostle. Maximilla has a similar companion in Iphidamia, with whom she visits the apostle Andrew. Mygdonia, Marcia and Tertia provide a final example of female friendship and sharing. When Mygdonia is to be baptized, she tells no one but her nurse Marcia, to whom she immediately turns, begging her to accompany her and be baptized too. In the same story, King Misdaeus sends his wife Terita to visit Mygdonia, knowing that she is more likely to convince Mygdonia to return to her husband than is he or any other man. Though his plan is unsuccessful, Misdaeus' assessment of the women's ability to persuade one another is accurate: when Tertia visits, Mygdonia tells her of her new faith, and Tertia decides to convert likewise.

A Woman's Point of View

It is likely that women living in the Hellenistic communities which produced the chastity stories would have told stories to one another. The question remains whether or not the chastity stories in particular would have been told by those women. On what basis can one identify these stories as women's stories, representative of a "woman's point of view"?

Folklorist Margaret Mills has studied contemporary oral narratives from a community in Afghanistan in which men and women are strictly segregated; she has found that "men tend to tell stories about men, whereas women tell stories about women and men."[13] Kay Stone, while studying the significance of fairy tales in our own culture, has discovered that very few men can remember female-dominated tales; and one nine-year-old boy who admitted to knowing the tales rejected them with the statement: "Those are girls' stories. They're about girls and not boys."[14]

The findings of Mills, Stone, and others indicate that the devaluation of the private female sphere leads men to avoid tales about women, whereas women are interested in both public and private spheres, stories with both male and female protagonists. This assymetry in the relationships of men and women to the public and private spheres has been well articulated by Jack Winkler in his study of the female poet Sappho:

> Insofar as men's public culture is truly public, displayed as the governing norm of social interaction "in the streets," it is accessible to women as well as men. Because men define and exhibit their langauge and manners as *the* culture and segregate women's language and manners as a subculture, inaccessible to and protected from extra-familial men, women are in the position of knowing two cultures while men know only one.[15]

The effects of the social and cultural structures which both separate public and private spheres and subordinate the private to the public are reinforced by the differences in the psychological development of men and women. Males define their gender identity primarily through creating boundaries and negating their identity with their mothers, while females, who have a less pressing need to separate from their mothers, develop "more flexible ego boundaries" and a greater ability to identify with others.[16] Hence women, while they may feel more strongly drawn to female characters, are also able to identify with male characters, whereas men have great difficulty identifying with female characters in folk narratives.

This principle has been utilized in scholarly attempts to identify a woman's point of view in anonymous works or even in works attributed to a man. Assuming that the one who tells and enjoys the story must be able to identify with the heroine or hero of that story, scholars have concluded that the concentration of a story on a female character or characters and the tendency to portray women more positively and in greater depth than men indicates a female viewpoint. Samuel Butler, in arguing for female authorship of the *Odyssey*, lays down the following guideline: "if in any work the women are found to be well and sympathetically drawn, while the men are mechanical and by comparison perfunctorily treated, it is, I imagine, safe to infer that the writer is a woman."[17] Invoking the same principle, Nora Chadwick suspects that certain Turkish poems in which the women are

> undoubtedly more gifted, both intellectually and spiritually, than their husbands and brothers . . . may have passed at some time through a feminine milieu, if they have not actually been composed by women.[18]

Arguing from the fact that several of the Hellenistic romantic novels focus primarily on the heroine rather than the hero, some have suggested that these novels were written by women, or at least that they had a predominately female audience.[19] Such arguments are perhaps incautious. Charles Beye has pointed out that the "strong feminine component" of the *Odyssey* seems to reflect a man's view of women rather than a woman's own sense of identity.[20] Likewise, Tomas Hagg questions "whether the image of Woman which the novels idealize--the beautiful, chaste and faithful-unto-death kind-

-is not rather a typically male product."[21] In the case of both the *Odyssey* and the novels, the stories offer male characters with whom men could conceivably identify, and it is questionable whether these works do indeed represent a "woman's point of view." However, if a story not only focuses on a heroine but also offers no satisfying males roles, its identity as a "woman's story" is more certain.

In the chastity stories, the primary male characters, husbands and governors, are not only villainous, but are unsuccessful in their villainy as well; even in the three stories where the husband is converted, he remains very much in the background, a shallow and weak character. In their present context in the apocryphal Acts of the apostles, the chastity stories might appear to offer a male reader the possibility of identification with the role of apostle. However, the structure of the chastity stories suggests that the apostle's original role in those particular stories was that of a "donor." He is no ordinary human being, but a quasi-magical figure who appears only so that he can present a "gift" to the heroine which will empower her to attain victory. Just as it would be unusual to identify with the "fairy godmother" in Cinderella or with the figure of Jesus in a miracle story, so it is unlikely that the early tellers of the chastity stories or their audiences identified with the role of apostle. The primary point of suspense in the story is not whether or not the apostle will triumph over the evil husband--we know that he will, for the husband has no power over the apostle, for whom even death is no threat. The primary point of suspense in the story is whether or not the woman, who is truly vulnerable, will escape the efforts of the husband to violate her chastity and prevent her from embracing the "new life" of the Christian. The woman, not the apostle, is the character with whom an audience is most likely to identify.

Focus on a positively portrayed heroine in the absence of a male protagonist with whom a man could identify suggests that the chastity stories are "women's stories." A closer look at the perspective from which the conflict of the chastity stories is presented confirms this view.[22] As Stevan Davies has noted,

> The great difficulty in Christian life is said time and time again to be the problem of continent living. This problem is always viewed from the standpoint of a woman who must leave her husband. At no time in the apocryphal Acts does a man encounter substantial difficulties in leaving his wife.[23]

To describe the woman's desertion of her husband from the husband's point of view, expressing sympathy for the plight of the husband, would fundamentally alter the structure and meaning of the story. Nor could the heroine simply be "replaced" by a hero. The "femaleness" of the heroine, her social and sexual identity and vulnerability as "wife," is crucial to the story. The stories center on conflict between male and female and present the male imposition as villainy, while focusing on the resistance of the heroine as the determining action of the stories.

The significance of sex roles for the meaning of the story is brought out with particular clarity in the Thecla version, which consistently arrays males on the side of the "villain," females on the side of the "heroine." While males threaten not only her chastity but her very life and even the apostle Paul deserts her in need, females--including a lioness--consistently support Thecla. The underlying hostility toward males communicated by the chastity stories suggests not only that a male would have difficulty identifying with their heroines but also that the stories were originally most likely told exclusively by and to women.[24]

Summary and Conclusions

The chastity stories originated in second-century Hellenistic communities of the eastern Mediterranean. Hellenistic society in general was characterized by a separation of male and female spheres, and the chastity stories themselves reflect a world in which women spent most of their time in the "private sphere" with other women, with whom they shared the stories of their own conversions. Modern folklore studies suggest that sex segregation leads to the formation of "sex specific" folklore, that is, distinct groups of "men's lore" and "women's lore." Hellenistic women are known for their story-telling, and we may safely assume that the women who lived in the communities which produced the chastity stories would have created and transmitted "women's stories."

Determining the original tellers and audiences of an ancient story is extremely difficult. However, studies of modern folklore suggest that men have difficulty identifying with female characters; they rarely tell or enjoy stories which focus on a woman protagonist and include no male heroes. It is therefore unlikely that men would have been the primary tellers or audiences of the chastity stories, which not only offer them no male characters with whom to identify but also express considerable hostility toward males.

We may conclude--however tentatively--that the chastity stories originated as "women's stories" and present a woman's point of view. The apostles, highly revered by first- and second-century Christians, feature prominently in these stories as "donor figures." Their presence in the chastity stories has proven fortuitous for women's history. Devotion to the apostles and curiosity about their lives caused these "private" women's stories to be incorporated into the Acts of the apostles and thus preserved in the "public" record of history--from which we, in turn, seek to reconstruct the "private" lives of the women storytellers.

Notes

[1] Dennis MacDonald, citing the support of Adolf von Harnack, suggests that the origin of the legend of Thecla may lie as far back as the first century; *The Legend and the Apostle*, pp. 17, 106, n.7.

[2] Claire R. Farrer, "Women and Folklore: Images and Genres," *Women and Folklore*, ed. Claire R. Farrer (Austin & London: Univ. of Texas Press, 1975), p. x.

[3] Heda Jason, *Conflict and Resolution in Jewish Sacred Tales* (Ann Arbor, Mich.: Univ. Microfilms Inc., 1968), p. 29.

[4] Farrer, p. xi.

[5] Jason, p. 41.

[6] Margaret R. Yocom, "Woman to Woman: Fieldwork and the Private Sphere," *Women's Folklore, Women's Culture*, ed. R. Jordan and S. Kalcik (Philadelphia: Univ. of Pennsylvania Press, 1985), p. 48.

[7] Achilles Tatius, *Clitophon and Leucippe*, p. 243.

[8] This quotation prefaces the telling of the story of Psyche by an old woman in a den of robbers. Compare the following passage from Xenophon's novel: "As those in Hippothoos' company [robbers] proceeded with their drinking, a certain old woman there present, named Chrision, began to tell a story" (*An Ephesian Tale*, p. 102).

[9] Farrer, p. xvi.

[10] See especially the *Lysistrata*, the *Thesmophoriazusae*, and the *Ecclesiazusae*.

[11] While the chastity stories are legends rather than historical accounts, the stories nevertheless reflect the world of their tellers in many ways. See pp. 84-87 below.

[12] *Acts of Peter*, Hennecke, *New Testament Apocrypha*, p. 316.

[13] Margaret Mills, "Sex Role Reversals, Sex Changes, and Transvestite Disguise in the Oral Tradition of a Conservative Muslim Community in Afghanistan," *Women's Folklore, Women's Culture*, p. 187.

[14] Kay F. Stone, "The Misuses of Enchantment: Controversies on the Significance of Fairy Tales," *Women's Folklore, Women's Culture*, p. 131.

[15] Jack Winkler, "Gardens of Nymphs: Public and Private in Sappho's Lyrics," *Reflections of Women in Antiquity*, ed. Helene P. Foley (NY, London, Paris: Gordon and Breach Science Publishers, 1981), pp. 68-9.

[16] Nancy Chodorow, "Family Structure and Feminine Personality," *Women, Culture and Society*, ed. M. Rosaldo and L. Lamphere (Stanford, CA: Stanford Univ. Press, 1974), p. 43; see also Carol Gilligan, *In a Different Voice* (Cambridge, MA and London: Harvard Univ. Press, 1982).

[17] Samuel Butler, *The Authoress of the Odyssey* (London: A. C. Fifield, 1897), p. 105.

[18] Nora K. Chadwick and Victor Zhirmunsky, *Oral Epics of Central Asia* (Cambridge: Univ. Press, 1969), p. 128.

[19] Hägg, *The Novel in Antiquity*, pp. 95-96.

[20] Charles Rowan Beye, "Male and Female in the Homeric Poems, " *Ramus* 3.2 (1974):87-101.

[21] Hägg, p. 96.

[22] There are numerous precedents for the attempt to identify a "woman's point of view" in a story through examination of the "perspective" from which a conflict is presented. In her interpretation of the *Hymn to Demeter*, Marilyn Arthur detects a "peculiarly feminine sensibility" in the *Hymn to Demeter*, which "treats the transition from 'matriarchy' to 'patriarchy' from the female point of view and therefore takes the form of a series of attempts to resist male domination rather than to impose it"; "Politics and Pomegranates: An Interpretation of the Homeric Hymn to Demeter," *Arethusa* 10.1 (1977):8. Folklorists studying living oral traditions have been able to identify the way perspective may shift when the same tale is told by a woman instead of a man. See for example Rosan Jordon's study of the tale of the "vaginal serpent." When told by women, this story emphasizes the "discomfort, helplessness and humiliation of the woman," who is assaulted and ultimately killed by the serpent. When told by men, the story emphasizes the threat represented by the woman's vagina, which is simultaneously a place where a serpent may get "lost" and a harborer of a dangerous "biting" creature. Rosan A. Jordon, "The Vaginal Serpent and Other Themes from Mexican-American Women's Lore," *Women's Folklore, Women's Culture*, pp. 26-33.

[23] Stevan L. Davies, *The Revolt of the Widows*, p. 63.

[24] There is evidence that both men and women tend to share their most hostile folk narratives with audiences of the same sex-- even when that hostility is not directed toward members of the other sex. See for example Carol Mitchell, "Some Differences in Male and Female Joke Telling," *Women's Folklore, Women's Culture*, pp. 163-86.

IV. A SOCIAL-HISTORICAL INTERPRETATION OF THE STORIES

The common structure shared by all of the chastity stories suggests that they were shaped by narrative concerns as well as by any historical events which they may describe; they are "legends," rather than "histories." However, even legends can yield historical information. First, many legends contain a historical "kernel": for instance, it is possible that there was a historical woman apostle named Thecla, and the legend gives us a clue to her existence. Second, the legend may indirectly reflect something about the historical situation of its tellers and audiences.

How does one extract the historical information from the legendary texts? How can either the historical "kernel" or the elements relating to the historical situation of the tellers be identified? One method is by comparison with other historical evidence from the same culture and period. If we know from Pliny's letter to Trajan[1] that persecutions of Christians in second-century Asia were initiated not by the Romans but by the local communities, then we have some grounds for believing that the chastity stories' presentation of the initiation of persecution of Christians by families and local communities is historically accurate.

A second method of identifying historical elements is by comparison with evidence from different cultures and periods which may be more accessible to study. Having observed how legends are informed by historical events and social institutions in modern cultures, we can tentatively assume that there would be analogous parallels between legends and historical events and social institutions in second-century Asia Minor or Syria or Greece. We can thus use models constructed on the basis of modern data in order to reconstruct the missing pieces of ancient history. This method is likely to highlight unique aspects of the second-century historical situation reflected in the chastity stories, whereas comparison with other data from second-century Christianity will reinforce what is already known about the period.

Our historical interpretation of the chastity stories will begin with a consideration of theories about the social and psychological functions of folk-stories and about the relation of the "narrative world" of the folk-story to the "real world" of history. These theories have been developed primarily on the basis of evidence from observable modern cultures. Applying these theories to the chastity stories, we will attempt to identify historical elements contained in the legends, confirming these through comparison with other evidence from the second century wherever possible.

Functions of the Folk-story: Theory

The functions of the folk-story are multiple; here we will consider briefly three of the most significant functions identified by folklore theorists.

The first is the "affective" function, which includes both "catharsis" and "wish fulfillment."[2]   The folk-story functions "cathartically" by enabling the expression of repressed emotions, whether in overt or disguised form, and thereby relieving the anxiety caused by the repression of these emotions. The folk-story also serves as wish fulfillment insofar as it enacts a pleasurable fantasy which is not being realized in the "real world." The affective function, in the form of both catharsis and wish fulfillment, is emphasized in psychoanalytic interpretations of folk-stories.

"Validation" of customs and institutions is another important function which has been recognized since Malinowski presented his well-known theory of myth as social "charter."[3] Folk-stories often serve to introduce, explain, and legitimate the practices and structures of a given society.

The function of "validation" is closely related to a third function, that of "motivation." "Motivation" involves maintaining conformity to the accepted practices and structures of society.

> More than simply serving to validate or justify institutions, beliefs and attitudes, some forms of folklore are important as means of applying social pressure and exercising social control. . . . [They are] employed against individuals who attempt to deviate from social conventions with which they are fully familiar.[4]

Folk-stories can "motivate" through positive inducements as well as through negative control; stories which express approval of those who conform serve this function.

All three of these functions are both psychological and social. While validation and motivation are described in primarily social terms, they also involve psychological processes of cognition and internalization of values, and they have significant effects on the individual psyche. Likewise, catharsis and wish fulfillment are described in primarily psychological terms but have significant social consequences as well. They can function as social mechanisms of "escape" and "compensation," providing outlets for frustration, dissatisfaction, or resentment, and thus stabilizing society by channelling potentially disruptive emotions in a relatively harmless direction. In this way the affective functions can join the validating and motivating functions in maintaining social stability.[5]

This socially stabilizing effect of folk-stories is stressed by most scholars, who rightly emphasize the interrelatedness of folklore and society: *individuals* do not generate or maintain folk-stories. However, folk-stories often interact with more than one "society," whereas social stability can be defined only from the point of view of a single society. Folklore may have a destabilizing effect from the point of view of one society at the same time that it has a stabilizing effect from the point of view of another. In particular, dissatisfied social groups may produce folk-stories which have a stabilizing effect on their own circles but a destabilizing effect on the larger societies in which they live.

> One of the most important functions of folklore is its service as a vehicle for social protest. Wherever there is injustice and oppression, one can be sure that the victims will find some solace in folklore.[6]

In this context, fantasizing or expressing repressed emotions serves not to dissipate but to heighten longings and frustrations. And validation and motivation serve to define and strengthen the identity and solidarity of a "society" of protestors.

'Narrative World" and 'Real World": Theory

The functions of the folk-story suggest that the story is likely to reflect some elements of the "real world" but may also contain both idealizations of reality and unreal elements of fantasy. J. L. Fischer phrases well the problems and the questions which arise out of the ambiguous relationship of folk-story to reality:

> One of the main problems in the attempt to fathom the significance of folktales is the imperfect correspondence and sometimes perverse opposition between the content of the tale and social reality.

> Is there a determinate relationship between folktales and social reality? If so, what aspects of social reality are related to folktale content, and how are they related--by exaggeration? by inversion? by direct reflection? How reliable are these relationships?[7]

While it is difficult to give conclusive answers to these questions, folklorists have developed some theoretical guidelines for determining the relationship between the narrative world of the folk-stories and the "real world" of history.

Lauri Honko has investigated ways in which folk narratives adapt themselves to cultural, social, economic, and physical factors of their environment.[8] These adaptations suggest how the historical situation of the tellers and audiences might be reflected in the stories. The two permanent adaptations which occur when a story enters a new environment are the "milieu-morphological" adaptation and the "tradition-morphological" adaptation.

In (1) milieu-morphological or "exterior" adaptation, a narrative undergoes familiarization and localization, i.e. the foreign natural setting is translated into the system of well-known features of the psychical milieu of the tradition community in question and the story is linked to a locality in the perceived environment. Among the processes of (2) tradition-morphological or "interior" adaptation there is the linking of role-figures of the narrative to well-known personages (tradition dominants), the censorship of tradition whereby elements which would lead to norm conflict are rejected or replaced, the adaptation of the narrative to a genre in a local or personal genre-system and to the genre-specific codes of communication.[9]

Thus we might expect a folk-story to reflect the familiar social and physical environment of the community in which it is told. We might also expect that the story would reflect the traditional norms and genres of the community, and that the role-figures might be identified with historical or legendary figures in the community's traditions.

Honko also mentions a third adaptation which is less enduring than the other two. He calls this the functional or "momentary/situational" adaptation; such an adaptation may occur every time a story is told.

> The personality of the narrator, the composition of the
> audience, the actual focus of interest of the community,
> events of the recent past and fears and hopes for the future, will normally intervene and bring about changes
> which lend the story a meaning *hic et nunc.*[10]

This adaptation suggests that a folk-story might reflect the particular concerns of its teller and audience in addition to the more general elements of cultural setting which it reflects in its first two adaptations.

The fourth and final adaptation which Honko lists, "ecotypification," is a broad concept which embraces the first three. Ecotypification is the adaptation of the folk-story to all cultural, social, economic, and natural factors of its environment.[11]

J. L. Fischer, like Honko, explores the ways in which the folk-story reflects the historical situation of its tellers and audiences; Fischer focuses most closely on the relationship of story to social conflict. He notes that folk-stories have a "selective concern with reality"[12] and finds that they tend to concentrate on difficult social transitions or relationships. Fischer concludes that it is safe to assume that any theme on which the folk-stories in a given society concentrate must be a subject of considerable conflict in that society.[13] Thus it is possible to infer a historical conflict from folk-stories. However, we cannot necessarily infer from the stories how the conflict was handled historically, since the resolution of the conflict in the story may represent either fantasy or reality, depending upon whether the story functioned as wish-fulfillment or as incitement to action.

Fischer also notes that folk-stories often describe real historical events, in addition to reflecting the conflicts with which their tellers and audiences are faced. Particularly when dramatic confrontations occur, the stories of these confrontations may be eagerly seized upon and told by people who feel themselves to be a part of similar if less dramatic conflicts.

> Real events of this extreme kind and the private fantasies relating to them become the focus for the formation of a folktale which will interest all of those who are involved in a similar conflict.[14]

The likelihood that a folk-story is based on real events is much higher in the case of legends than of folktales or myths, since only legends claim to be directly concerned with real people and real events taking place in the recent past. Also, legends are generated much more readily and frequently than are folktales and myths and tend to be more variable and thus more responsive to historical realities, both on the level of the original shaping of the story, and on the level of adaptation to audiences and tellers.

Historical Realities Reflected in the Chastity Stories: Application of Theory

(a) Boundaries of the woman's world

According to Honko's theory of adaptations, the folk narrative tends to conform itself to the familiar setting, traditions, and concerns of the community in which it is told. We see hints of such adaptations in the differences between variants of the chastity story: names of towns are changed, titles as well as names of governing officials vary, and the characters filling the roles of woman, husband, and apostle shift. The names of governor, woman, and husband may very well be taken from characters already established in the community's traditions; certainly that is the case with the apostle, whose role is linked with the particular apostle who plays the most important part in the traditions of the community--the "tradition dominant" apostle.

Other elements are constant throughout all variants of the chastity story; some of these reflect aspects of the tellers' environment which were common to all of the communities where the

stories were told. One such common element has already been
mentioned in the discussion of the stories' tellers: the existence of
a distinct "female sphere." Because the chastity stories tell of
women who offend their societies by transgressing the boundaries
of the woman's sphere, they call attention to the location of those
boundaries.

In the *Acts of Thomas*, Mygdonia, accompanied by her
slaves, leaves her house to visit the apostle Thomas. When she
returns home, her husband Charisius asks her, "Why didst thou
not have regard to thy position as a free woman and remain in thy
house but go out and listen to vain words and look upon magic
works?"[15] Charisius has a reputation as a "hard man . . . who will
not allow her to continue in this opinion."[16]   Nevertheless,
Mygdonia leaves the house again. Moreover, when her husband
attempts to sleep with her, she flees from him and goes to sleep
with her nurse. Charisius laments her strange behavior and expresses his worst fears and suspicions: that she may have left the
house and be involved in unchaste relations with another man.

> Noble lady that she is, whom none of her house ever
> charged with impropriety, she has fled naked from her
> chamber and run outside, and I know not where she has
> gone. And perhaps, maddened by that sorcerer, she has
> in her frenzy gone into the marketplace in search of
> him.[17]

Later in the story, Mygdonia does actually sneak out of the house
alone at night to visit the apostle. When she persists in defying his
orders that she not visit the apostle, Charisius locks her up inside.
However, God miraculously releases her from her confinement.

Artemilla also leaves her house, accompanied by a female
friend, and visits an apostle. Her husband hears of it and is "not a
little wroth."[18] Artemilla, like Mygdonia, goes so far as to sneak
out at night to be baptized by Paul. Afterwards, Paul sends her
home "to her husband."[19]

Maximilla not only sneaks out of the house regularly with her servant Iphidamia to visit the apostle Andrew--she also invites the apostle into her home and her very bedroom. Her husband Aegeates tries in vain to prevent these outrages by imprisoning Andrew and placing guards outside his wife's room. Distraught at his wife's refusal to share his bed, Aegeates questions Andrew, "Why did you think it good to force your way into places which were no concern of yours and to corrupt a wife prior to that satisfied me?"[20] His household has been "destabilized," and he is unable to restore it to order or enforce its boundaries. After Andrew's crucifixion, Maximilla continues to defy convention by appearing in public : "Maximilla came with Stratocles without a thought of those who were standing around and took down the body of Andrew."[21] She then permanently separates from Aegeates and his house. "She chose a holy and quiet life which she, full of the love of Christ, spent among the brethren."[22]

Thecla, unlike the other women, initially does not dare to leave the house: she sits at a window and listens to the apostle Paul from a distance. Her stationary location inside the house is in marked contrast to her fiance's movement and activity in the outside world. When Thecla does finally leave the house, she does so secretly and at night, slipping away alone to visit Paul in prison. Her transgression is discovered, and the citizens of her town are so outraged that they request that the governor punish her. Having left her house, Thecla confirms her defiance by refusing to marry Thamyris. The governor sentences her to be burned, but Thecla escapes and commences a life of wandering in the outside world. Her free movement seems to imply to men that she is sexually promiscuous, for Alexander does not hesitate to molest her on the street. She escapes from him and henceforth remains free from men and their houses; the only houses she enters are those of women.

In all of the stories, it is clear that the woman's proper place is in the inner world of her husband's house, while the husband moves in the outer, public world. By remaining in the house, the woman accepts her place in society, marriage, and sexual relationships. When she leaves the house, she is crossing boundaries, intruding into the male world and provoking disapproval, hostility, and suspicion of infidelity. Sometimes she leaves secretly or at night, which underlines the suspiciousness of her behavior. By defying the physical boundaries of her proper sphere, she is also defying the boundaries of the social-sexual role assigned to her within the institution of patriarchal marriage: she leaves the house, and leaves the husband's rule.

The *crossing* of boundaries does not necessarily represent the historical experience of the tellers; it may instead reflect their fantasies. However, following Honko's theory of "milieu-morphological adaptations," we can assume that the boundaries themselves are patterned after the social structures and behavioral norms of the communities in which the stories were told. There is ample evidence external to the chastity stories to confirm the separation of "public male" and "private female" spheres within Hellenistic society. The following Neopythagorean treatise, written near the beginning of the Hellenistic period, clearly articulates this separation of spheres:

> Men should be generals and city officials and politicians, and women should keep house and stay inside and receive and take care of their husbands. . . . Courage and intelligence are more appropriately male qualities because of the strength of men's bodies and the power of their minds. *Sophrosyne*[23] is more appropriately female. Accordingly a woman must learn about *sophrosyne* and realise what she must do quantitatively and qualitatively to be able to obtain this womanly virtue. I believe that there are five qualifications: (1) the sanctity of her mar-

riage bed (2) the cleanliness of her body (3) the manner in which she chooses to leave her house (4) her refusal to participate in secret cults or Cybeline rituals (5) her readiness and moderation in sacrificing to the gods.[24]

Here, as in the chastity stories, womanly virtue includes not only maintaining sexual fidelity to a husband but also dressing with modesty (i.e., protecting the privacy of her body) and remaining within the private sphere of the household. Indeed, as aspects of the same virtue, sexual fidelity and privacy are essentially equated, so that when a woman leaves the house it is often assumed that she is sexually unfaithful to her husband. Thus, when Alexander sees Thecla walking in the streets of Antioch, he concludes that she is unchaste. Likewise, when Charisius believes Mygdonia has fled from the house naked, he immediately fears that she is sexually involved with Thomas.

Though she ideally remains at home, a virtuous woman may leave the house on occasion. The Neopythagorean treatise elaborates the conditions under which such an expedition might occur:

> Women of importance leave the house to sacrifice to the leading divinity of the community on behalf of themselves and their husbands and their households. They do not leave home at night nor in the evening, but at midday, to attend a religious festival or to make some purchase, accompanied by a single female servant or decorously escorted by two servants at most. . . . They keep away from secret cults and Cybeline orgies in their homes. For public law prevents women from participating in these rites, particularly because these forms of worship encourage drunkenness and ecstasy.[25]

A virtuous woman may leave her home if it is midday, she is accompanied by one or two female servants, and her purpose is either to attend an appropriate religious festival or to go shopping.

Again, these prescriptions for women's behavior are in accord with the chastity stories. There we hear of women leaving home at mid-day in the company of female slaves or friends: Xanthippe and the prefect's concubines leave the house together, Mygdonia goes out in a litter accompanied by several slaves, Artemilla is accompanied on her outing by her friend Eubula, and Maxmilla by her friend Iphidamia. These daylight excursions do not in themselves arouse disapproval or hostility; however, the chastity stories suggest that a woman who goes out is incurring some risk of falling under "dangerous" influences. It is on their journeys into the public world that the women meet the apostles.

Initially, the apostle's position as religious leader is am-biguous in relation to the woman's sphere: we have seen that reli-gion is considered an appropriate concern of a virtuous woman, and offers one of the few legitimate reasons for a woman to leave the house; on the other hand, women are forbidden to take part in "secret cults" or "magic," i.e., any religion which is viewed as a threat to the social or political orders. The ambiguity is soon re-solved: in the view of the husband and governor, the apostle is a "magician" or "sorcerer," and his religion is not one with which a virtuous woman concerns herself. When the woman not only con-tinues to visit the apostle after the husband expresses his disap-proval, but does so alone and at night, as do Thecla, Mygdonia, Tertia, and Artemilla, she has clearly transgressed the boundaries of the woman's sphere.

The chastity stories share with other Hellenistic writings the depiction of a social world in which the boundaries of a private "woman's sphere" are clearly defined. That woman's sphere was centered in the household and in the woman's duties as wife. The physical boundaries between the inner world of the house and the outer, public world were not utterly impassible; when accompanied by female companions and when attending religious festivals, women were permitted to leave the house. However, frequent or nocturnal forays into the public sphere were discouraged and interpreted as improper and even defiant behavior.

(b) Political backing of the social order

A second aspect of the narrative world of the stories which likely reflects the world of their tellers is the role which the Roman government plays in backing the social order of the communities. In the chastity stories, this social order is above all the order of marriage and household, in which the woman's position is well defined and well bounded. When this social order is threatened, the prominent citizens call upon the Roman governor to protect it. Thus marriage becomes a political as well as a social concern.

In the story of Thecla, Thamyris, an influential citizen, gathers the "rulers and officers and a great crowd" of his fellow Iconians and goes before the governor--in this case a proconsul--and charges Paul with teaching maidens not to marry.[26] The governor imprisons Paul. Shortly thereafter, Thecla visits Paul in prison, and Thamyris and his crowd again go to the governor and beg him to take action. The governor questions Thecla, "Why dost thou not marry Thamyris according to the law of the Iconians?"[27] When Thecla refuses to answer, her own mother urges the governor to "burn the lawless one."[28] The governor tries to comply, but Thecla miraculously escapes.

In the second episode of Thecla's story, Alexander, another influential citizen, likewise appeals to a Roman governor when Thecla repulses his sexual advances. Again, the governor complies with the citizen's request for punishment: he condemns Thecla to the beasts.

In the story of Xanthippe, Albinus, a "friend of Caesar,"[29] convinces the prefect to execute the "troublemaker" who has been teaching wives to leave their husbands.[30] In this story, however, the offense has escalated, for the prefect's own concubines have left him as well; thus patriarchal marriage and politics become very closely linked indeed. Similarly, in the story of Artemilla and

Eubula, though it is the governor's freedman who originally incites the governor to persecute the apostle Paul, when the governor's own wife becomes a disciple of Paul, the governor is directly involved in defending his own marriage. The story of Mygdonia follows the same pattern. Finally, in the stories of Maximilla, Tertia, and the "princess bride," the husband/father *is* the political ruler, and there are no intervening figures.

The Augustan legislation on marriage, which remained in effect for the first three centuries of the Christian era, provides dramatic evidence external to the chastity stories that the Roman government had considerable interest in backing the institution of patriarchal marriage. The *Lex Julia de maritandis ordinibus* and *Lex Papia Poppea* penalized the unmarried and childless, as well as widows or divorced women who failed to remarry within two years. Though the motives behind the Augustan legislation are debated, the laws clearly demonstrate that marriage was not voluntarily chosen by all of the women and men living under the Roman Empire, and that their refusal to marry was viewed not only as a departure from ancient tradition but also as a threat to the political order.[31]

(c) Social-political conflict

Following Honko's emphasis on how the immediate concerns of tellers and audiences mold folk-stories, as well as Fischer's assertion that folk-stories focus on subjects of real conflict in the societies in which they are told, we might make a third judgement about the historical experience of the tellers and audiences of the chastity stories: the tellers and audiences were women who experienced tension within the institution of patriarchal marriage and who felt themselves to be in conflict with the social and political powers which backed this institution.

The very structure of the chastity story presents the husband and the political ruler as villains and opponents of the woman. Moreover, the details in each variant story emphasize the woman's remarkable lack of sympathy for her husband's plight. While Charisius weeps and pleads his love eloquently and tenderly, Mygdonia sits "silent and looking on the ground."[32]   When she finally replies, it is to reject Charisius with a devastating finality:

He whom I love is better than thee and thy possessions.
For thy possession is of the earth and returns to earth;
but he whom I love is heavenly, and will take me with
him into heaven. Thy wealth shall pass away, and thy
beauty shall vanish, and thy robes and thy many works;
but thou (shalt) remain alone with thy transgressions . . .
. Remind me not of thy deeds toward me.[33]

Thecla likewise is very ready to reject and humiliate the men who love and admire her, and her story does not present any male positively; even male animals are her opponents, while female animals give her aid. Finally, Maximilla calmly drives her husband to suicide, and his death represents the "happy ending" of her story.

It might be argued that the women who told the chastity stories seem to be concerned with ascetic purity and salvation in the afterlife, rather than with patriarchal social structures. Their defiance of marriage and their hostility toward men might be seen merely as an accidental result of their striving for salvific self-denial. Arguing against this point of view is the fact that the stories never describe chastity in terms of self-denial; not once does a woman in these stories lament her renunciation of sexual relations--though the husbands frequently do. Nor are ascetic purity and the hope of the afterlife ever presented outside the context of social conflict. In these stories, Christian life style and hope are inseparable from conflict with the institution and defenders of patriarchal marriage. Conflict with the old society is a necessary and important consequence of embracing the new.

(d) Active and triumphant defiance

The three factors described above--the boundaries of the woman's world, political backing of the social order, and the existence of social-political conflict between women and the social order--can be interpreted with some confidence as direct reflections of the social world of the tellers. However, there are other aspects of the stories which cannot be accepted as historically accurate descriptions without further discussion. Among the most significant of these is the mode of resolution of the conflict. Does the active and triumphant defiance of the women reflect reality or fantasy? Another way to pose this question is: Did the telling of the story function as a socially stabilizing "outlet" or as a destabilizing incitement to protest? These questions touch upon the historical interpretation of both the subject of the story (i.e., Maximilla's conflict with Aegeates) and the world of its tellers, which may represent two historically distinct phenomena. These two levels of possible historical interpretation further complicate the answers to questions which are already complex. In the discussion below, I cannot hope to present unassailable historical "facts"; my intention is simply to weave my way through some of the major issues and possible interpretations and to point out what seem to be the most reasonable and likely historical reconstructions.

Were there historical second-century women who were inspired by Christianity to defy their husbands, families, and societies and even their political rules by renouncing marriage? Or are the stories of dramatic defiance mere fantasies? Some of the stories may have been embroidered significantly, and perhaps some became attached to the names of well-known women who actually had no such experiences. It is, however, unlikely that the chastity stories represent complete fabrications. There is historical evidence external to the stories which suggests that some Christian women did indeed leave their husbands. The following account from Justin Martyr's *Second Apology*, which is contemporary with the chastity stories, provides a particularly close parallel:

A certain woman lived with an intemperate (*akolastainonti*) husband; she herself, too, having formerly been intemperate. But when she came to the knowledge of the teachings of Christ she became sober-minded, and endeavoured to persuade her husband likewise to be temperate . . . . But he, continuing in the same excesses, alienated his wife from him by his actions. For she . . . wished to be divorced from him. And when she was overpersuaded by her friends, who advised her still to continue with him, . . . she did violence to her own feeling and remained with him. But when her husband had gone to Alexandria, and was reported to be conducting himself worse than ever, she . . . gave him what you call a bill of divorce, and was separated from him. But this noble husband of hers . . . , when she had gone from him without his desire, brought an accusation against her, affirming that she was a Christian. And she presented a paper to thee, the Emperor, requesting that first she be permitted to arrange her affairs, and afterwards to make her defence against the accusation, when her affairs were set in order. And this you granted. And her *quondam* husband, since he was now no longer able to prosecute her, directed his assaults against a man, Ptolemaeus whom Urbicus punished, and who had been her teacher in the Christian doctrine.[34]

This woman, like the women depicted in the chastity stories, converted to Christianity and a "temperate" or "chaste" life style--though it is not clear from Justin's account whether she renounced sexual relations with her husband altogether. Because her husband refused to convert to the new belief and ways, she separated from him. Her husband brought charges against her before Roman law, but she obtained temporary immunity from the charges. Her husband then brought charges against her teacher,

who, like the apostles of the chastity stories, was imprisoned and
punished. Justin does not mention whether the woman was ever
convicted and punished.

It is likely that historical events such as the one related by
Justin Martyr would have appealed to the imaginations of many
women, who would have told and retold the stories with great plea-
sure. Recall Fischer's description of how folk narratives are often
formed:

> Real events of this extreme kind, and the private fan-
> tasies relating to them, become the focus for the forma-
> tion of a folktale which will interest all of those who are
> involved in a similar conflict.[35]

"Real events" may well have inspired some versions of the chastity
stories in their presentation of Christian women actively defying
their husbands.

The historical experience of leaving a husband might have
been shared not only by the subjects but also by the tellers of the
stories. That is to say, the chastity stories might have originally
been told primarily by and to Christian women who had left their
husbands. Such women would have continued to encounter opposition to their life style, and the telling of the chastity stories would
have served to encourage them in their struggles and to strengthen
their sense of purpose and identity. Not all of the women who enjoyed the stories would have experienced as dramatic a conflict as
did the subjects of the stories, and some of the tellers might be
widows or virgins rather than divorced women (even among the
subjects of the stories, Thecla is a virgin, and Maximilla is eventually widowed); but all would feel the conflict and the pressure to
conform to the dominant social conventions and to become a part
of a patriarchal household. The Christian beliefs and the ascetic
life style shared by such women would have defined them as a distinct social group, and the chastity stories would have functioned

to validate beliefs and practices and to motivate proper life style within this group.

But we cannot assume close historical parallels between the lives of the subjects and the lives of the tellers in all cases. It is possible that the chastity stories were also enjoyed by women who were neither single nor Christian. In this context, the stories would function to allow women to express their repressed hostilities, resentments, or dissatisfaction, and to fantasize about defiance of husbands and freedom from marriage; the stories would function to provide catharsis and wish-fulfillment. Perhaps many of the chastity stories' tellers and audiences were women who would not actually take the step of leaving their husbands and/or converting to Christianity. But by encouraging the women's expressiveness and fantasies, the stories might have functioned as incitement to rebellion. Conversion stories are often told to win converts, and we might expect the chastity stories to have served this missionary function as well.

(e) Social class

All of the heroines of the chastity stories are portrayed as upper-class women. Xanthippe is the wife of an influential Roman citizen who is a friend of Caesar. Thecla describes herself as one of the first among the Iconians. Maximilla and Artemilla are the wives of governors, and Drusiana's husband also seems to be an influential citizen. The bride in the *Acts of Thomas* is a princess, and Tertia is a king's wife, while Mygdonia is the wife of a wealthy and influential friend of the king. Is the high social status of these women likely reflective of historical reality? If so, would it apply to the tellers and audiences as well as the subjects of the stories?

There are at least two reasons to question the historicity of this aspect of the stories. First, it is extremely common for folk-stories to exaggerate social status and to focus on upper-class subjects. Second, it is possible that the chastity story might originally have existed independently of the martyrdom story--though no examples of such an independent version have survived. Whereas the chastity story focuses on the conflict between the woman and the husband or lover, the martyrdom story--which does exist in independent form--focuses on the conflict between the apostle and the governor. When these stories are brought together, husband and governor tend to merge in the "villain" role, and this merging of husband with governor might account for the fact that the woman and her husband are always members of the ruling class in the chastity-martyrdom stories.

There are also good reasons to accept the historicity of the women's high social class. By the late second century, Christianity had begun to reach the upper levels of Greco-Roman society, and there its greatest and earliest success seems to have been among women. During the Hellenistic and imperial periods, women's economic rights and powers had expanded significantly and many women exerted considerable political influence through their roles as mothers, daughters, and wives of politically powerful men;[36] but they nevertheless remained marginal in public life. "They cannot partake of magistracies, priesthoods, triumphs, badges of office, gifts, or spoils of war," remarks Livy in a speech he attributes to Lucius Valerius (*History of Rome* 34.7). Even the formidable Livia, wife of Augustus, "never ventured to enter the senate-chamber of the camps or the public assemblies," according to the historian Dio (*Roman History* 57.12). The discrepancy between women's experience of their own power and ability, on the one hand, and their awareness of their lack of public status and political opportunity, on the other, may have been a major factor in leading upper-class women to seek status and leadership positions in religion, the only "semi-public" realm to which women were freely admitted.[37] Many women were actively involved not only in the more traditional religions of Greece and Rome, but also in the "newer" and more exotic religions of the east: the mystery cults, Judaism, and Christianity. [38]

Given the general attraction of Christianity for upper-class women, it is quite possible that some of the women who sought out the single life would have been upper-class women or at least women of substantial means. Due to the folk preference for upper-class heroines, the stories would tend to focus on such women and even to exaggerate their social status. As the chastity stories were joined to martyrdom stories, they would also tend to link the women with the wives of the Roman governors who persecuted the apostles, intensifying the depiction of the woman's high social status. Though the stories focus on upper-class women, women from a wide range of social classes probably told the stories. Indeed, to the extent that high social status is emphasized rather than accepted as normative, the stories may indicate that most of their tellers did not share the social status of the heroines.

> When the poetic fantasy turns to kings, landowners and
> the rich, is that the fantasy of kings, landowners and the
> rich, or of those who are excluded from these upper so-
> cial brackets? Fairy tales and the sensational press in
> our own day show that the latter is also a possibility.[39]

A slight confirmation of the view that the tellers included women from lower as well as upper social classes is offered by the fact that the stories themselves give a very positive portrayal of women from a variety of social classes. Thecla shares her teachings with the wealthy Tryphaena as well as with Tryphaena's maidservants, Mygdonia shares her Christianity with a servant woman and a king's wife, and the "princess bride" welcomes a flute-girl into her home.

(f) Women's communities

It is tempting to speculate further about the life style of the women who actually left their families. Stevan Davies hypothesizes that these women would have belonged to the groups of so-called "widows" who were supported by the organized structure of the patriarchal church.[40] If some of them were independently wealthy, it is also possible that the wealthier women supported the poorer women, as Tryphaena seems to have supported Thecla. Whatever their source of financial support, it is likely that the women who had separated from their families would have found new "families" in communities of single Christian women.

Traditional histories of the ascetic communities in early Christianity begin with Antony, the "founder of monasticism." However, there were single women living together in Christian community before Antony; it was with these "well-known and faithful virgins" that Antony left his sister before embarking upon his own ascetic career around the year 270 C.E.[41] Unfortunately, evidence for women's communities before this date is scanty, and it is difficult to know how far back the practice goes, how widespread the women's communities were, whether they stood in close connection to one another, or what their relationship was with other parts of the church. Two texts from the beginning of the second century refer to women living in community. *1 Timothy* 5:16 directs that Christian women who have widows living with them should continue to support them, rather than burden the church. Likewise, Ignatius of Antioch sends greetings to the "virgins called widows" in Smyrna and seems to indicate that these women live in households which are separate from the households of Christian families (*Letter to the Smyrnaeans* 13). The apocryphal Acts, compiled later in the second century, often mention "widows" as a collective group, and at least one passage indicates clearly that these women lived together.[42] Letters attributed to Clement of Rome, probably also written in the late second century, refer to the "houses of virgin brothers and sisters" (*First Epistle Concerning Virginity* 10); these may have been houses in which ascetics lived in community.

It is often assumed that women before the fourth century lived with their families under the authority of their fathers, but it is possible that women's communities go back at least as far as the second century. It is intriguing to speculate--though difficult to prove--that the women who told the chastity stories might have lived together in communities which embraced women of all ages and classes and which may have been supported not by the institutions of the patriarchal church, as Davies suggests, but by the wealthy women among them.

(g) Role of the apostle

One last major element of the chastity stories remains to be interpreted historically: the role of the apostle. Several possible interpretations have been suggested, all of which may contain some degree of truth. The first interpretation is the simplest and also the least plausible: the figures of the apostles in the chastity stories stem primarily from memories of the historical apostles. While this possibility cannot be completely ruled out, it is unlikely that memories of the original apostles significantly inform the chastity stories, which were told a century or more after the deaths of these apostles, and which depict the apostles' martyrdoms in historically improbable conformity with one another.

A second and perhaps more promising interpretation is that the apostles in the chastity stories are modelled upon itinerant Christian preachers of the second century. Stevan Davies presents this theory in some detail. Davies notes that there are several second-century references to wandering preachers, but that little is known about them, aside from what the apocryphal Acts may reveal.

> From the apocryphal Acts we can, perhaps, learn how they were viewed by persons who respected or revered them, but this evidence can at best lead us to assess probabilities rather than to draw firm conclusions.[43]

Admitting the hypothetical nature of his reconstruction, Davies goes on to interpret the portraits of the apostle-preachers with reference both to contemporary views of magic and wonder-workers and to modern sociological theories about charismatic leadership. Davies finds that

> the virtue of the apostle lies in his opposition . . . to so-
> cial life in general and in the concomitant capacity for
> self-control that enabled such an asocial existence to be
> endured.[44]

However, the apostle's mission is to convert others to Christianity and to create a community of believers, and there is a tension between the asocial virtues upheld by the apostle and the communal life style which the apostle functions to create.

> The Christian social structure that emerges at least par-
> tially because of the activities of the apostle will have to
> be one which to some extent rejects the asocial virtues of
> the apostles and, therefore, disowns the apostles them-
> selves.[45]

Davies believes that the women who told the chastity stories (and other stories of the apocryphal Acts) would have been adherents of the itinerant preachers but financially dependent on the local Christian community, which was already becoming "both institutional and patriarchal";[46] the women were thus caught at a point of tension between wandering preachers and stable communities. According to Davies, the Acts were written in a period of transition, and the apostle-preachers represent the last wave of charismatic leadership before the final triumph of institutional leadership.

While Davies' interpretation is plausible, it depends upon the methodological assumption that "in writing pious fiction people model the imaginative world about which they write on the real social world in which they live."[47] This assumption needs to be qualified by the recognition that some functions of story-telling may distort the representation of the "real social world" in which the tellers live.

A third interpretation of the apostle's role emphasizes the folk-story's function of "validation" or "legitimation." As discussed above, the chastity stories probably served in part to legitimate the unmarried life style of the women who told the stories. Legitimation could function both internally, to inform and strengthen the identity and life style of the community, and externally, to persuade potential converts and to defend the women's lifestyle against outside disapproval. Given the extreme importance placed on apostolic authority in early Christianity, the apostle's role in the story would surely have been crucial to this legitimating function. Dennis MacDonald has produced concrete evidence for the legitimating role of the apostle in the Thecla story. This story seems to have been told in the context of the conflict between rival communities, both of which claimed Paul's authority for their differing life styles and doctrines. One of these communities produced pseudepigraphal letters in Paul's name (the Pastoral Epistles), while the other produced stories about Paul (the Thecla story and others incorporated into the *Acts of Paul*); both used Paul to legitimate their own values and beliefs.[48] It is reasonable to assume that the role of the apostle would have functioned similarly in the other chastity stories. If this is the case, it is not *necessary* to posit the existence of apostle-like figures in the world of the tellers, as does Davies, in order to explain the presence of the apostles in the stories.

The function of legitimation does not, however, account for all aspects of the apostle's role; in particular, it does not account for the element of "erotic substitution" which has inspired so many scholars to read the chastity stories as Hellenistic romantic novels. While the novelistic stories and the chastity stories are structurally distinct and represent historically independent story types, the chastity stories do share with the novels a stereotype of romantic love and a set of motifs which cluster around this stereotype. Of these "erotic" motifs, the motif of the jealous husband appears most consistently throughout the chastity stories and hints at a romantic dimension to the relationship between the woman and the apostle. The Thecla story describes Thecla as being "bound with [Paul] in affection"[49] and repeatedly emphasizes Thecla's longing for and devotion to Paul. And the stories of Mygdonia and Tertia and the Princess Bride, all from the *Acts of Thomas*, explicitly portray the relationship of the woman to the apostle (who is identified with Christ) as a new "marriage" which replaces her old marriage to her husband. While these suggestions of eroticism in the relationship between the woman and the apostle should not be overemphasized, they also cannot be dismissed.

Those who posit a literary relationship between the Acts and the novel naturally view the erotic elements as concessions to the novelistic genre, perhaps consciously introduced to give the stories popular appeal. Such a view is not necessarily inconsistent with the claim that the chastity stories originated as folk-stories independent of the novel, for the novelistic elements might have been introduced by the redactors who put the stories into literary form; they would thus represent later "corruptions" of the pure Christian stories. There is, however, no clear justification for the separation of the erotic elements from the rest of the stories. Indeed, the jealousy of the husband toward the apostle and the woman's transferral of love and faithfulness from her husband to the apostle and/or Christ seem to be basic to the stories.

Davies would claim that the traces of eroticism in the stories reflect the historical relationships of the women storytellers with the wandering preachers to whom they were strongly emotionally attached. But it might equally be true that the stories reflect the fantasies which the women tellers projected onto the legendary figures of the apostles and/or Christ. Whether in fantasy or in real relationships, the women seem to have rechannelled or "sublimated" their sexual energies in their new spiritual relationship with Christ, as represented by the apostle. Such sublimation would be facilitated by the emphasis on the metaphor of Christ as "bridegroom." The role of the apostle thus has a psychological function as well as a function of social legitimation.

In pursuing the psychological function of the apostle's role in somewhat more detail, I would point to parallels between the apostle and donor figures in fairy tales. Donors are often identified with the parent, and specifically with positive images of the parent. Thus, in the story of Cinderella the "real mother" or the "fairy god-mother" represents a child's positive projections of her or his mother, while the "stepmother" embodies the negative projections. Similarly, the apostle in the chastity story reflects the women's positive projections of father/husband figures, while the husband reflects the negative projections. The husband is the restrictive authority, the one who does not understand,the one whose sexuality is threatening. The apostle, in contrast, is empowering and supportive, understanding, and sexually attractive. Bruno Bettel-heim maintains that it is the unconscious hope of finding the positive father or mother figure "which gives us the strength to leave home."[50] Thus, fantasies which build this hope aid in the development of independence from the parent. In breaking away from marriage, the women tellers of the chastity stories underwent a process similar to that of a child separating from parents. Their relationship to the apostle (whether in reality or fantasy) must have helped to give them the strength to "leave home." Likewise, their projection of all negative feelings toward males onto their husbands would have aided them in breaking away. It is noteworthy that the stories acknowledge that the apostles cannot actually accomplish the transition for the women, or even assist them in any way beyond giving them the empowering "gift"; the apostles remain on the sidelines of the woman's struggle, and their stay with her is temporary.

Recognition of these social and psychological functions of the apostle's role has direct bearing on historical intepretation insofar as it affects the assessment of the historicity of the chastity stories' presentation of the apostles. It is possible that the stories contain memories of some first-century women who were converted to Christianity and chastity by the original apostles, and still more probable that the stories reflect the experience of some second-century women who were converted to Christianity and chastity by itinerant preachers. However, I would view the apostle's story role as being primarily shaped not by the subjects' or tellers' actual relationships with these apostles and preachers, but rather by the tellers' concerns to legitimate their life style and beliefs and by their need to break away psychologically from their dependence on their husbands or families.

Summary and Conclusions

The chastity stories are witnesses of the experiences of second-century eastern Christian women who lived in societies in which women's roles were clearly defined within the structures of patriarchal marriage and household. These women found their roles to be limiting and unsatisfying and thus felt themselves to be in some conflict with the social and political institutions which enforced the definition of their roles. Some of them were inspired and encouraged by Christian teaching to renounce marriage, even when this involved open defiance of the dominant social and political institutions. Some may have lived together in communities, which would probably have included women from a variety of social classes. They told stories of their heroic and defiant fore-sisters. They felt themselves to be united with Christ in a liberating relationship which surpassed and excluded their previous familial and marital relationships.

These conclusions are based on reconstructions of the world behind the legends, reconstructions which are in turn grounded in modern theories of folklore and supported by historical evidence external to the stories. Such conclusions are necessarily tentative; however, they are no less tentative than other theories about women in antiquity. Such conclusions are also necessarily lacking in precision as to dates, places, and persons involved; but insofar as they accurately describe the experiences and attitudes of the "folk," their imprecision reflects the diffusion of the phenomena, not the inaccuracy of the method.

Finally, however tentative or imprecise these bits of historical data may be, their rareness imbues them with great value. They remind us that second- century Christianity was not exclusively a man's affair, and that the absence of women's voices in most surviving early Christian texts does not necessarily imply the silence of early Christian women. There were passionate, suffering, dreaming, independent, and defiant women among second-century Christians, and these women are part of the history and heritage of all Christians.

Notes

1 Pliny, *Letter to Trajan* X.xcvi.

2 J. L. Fischer, "The Sociopsychological Analysis of Folktales," *Current Anthropology* 4.3 (June 1963):257. See also William Bascom, "Four Functions of Folklore," *The Study of Folklore*, ed. A. Dundes (Englewood Cliffs, NJ, 1965), p. 290.

3 Malinowski, *Myth in Primitive Psychology* (NY, 1926). See also Bascom, p. 292; Fischer, pp. 259-60.

4 Bascom, p. 294.

5 Ibid., pp. 290, 297; Fischer, p. 259.

6 Alan Dundes, *The Study of Folklore*, p. 308.

7 Fischer, pp. 239, 261.

8 Lauri Honko, "Methods in Folk-Narrative Research," *Ethnologia Europaea* 11 (1979/80):23-25.

9 Ibid., p. 23.

[10] Ibid., p. 24.

[11] Ibid, pp. 24-25.

[12] Fischer, pp. 261-62.

[13] Ibid., p. 262.

[14] Ibid., p. 263.

[15] *Acts of Thomas*, Hennecke, p. 490.

[16] *Acts of Thomas*, ibid., pp. 491, 496.

[17] *Acts of Thomas*, ibid., p. 494.

[18] *Acts of Paul*, ibid., p. 371.

[19] *Acts of Paul*, ibid., p. 372.

[20] *Acts of Andrew*, ibid., pp. 416-17.

[21] *Acts of Andrew*, ibid., p. 423.

[22] *Acts of Andrew*, ibid.

[23] *Sophrosyne*, often translated "chastity," here refers to sexual fidelity to a husband--among other virtues. I have retained the Greek form in order to distinguish it from the use of the English word "chastity," which elsewhere in this work refers to sexual abstinence within marriage as well as without. See introduction, p. 4, n. 4.

[24] Neopythagorean treatise translated in Mary R. Lefkowitz and Maureen B. Fant, *Women's Life in Greece and Rome* (Baltimore: The Johns Hopkins Univ. Press, 1982), p. 104; for original Greek, see *The Pythagorean Texts of the Hellenistic Period*, ed., H. Thesleff (Abo, 1965), pp. 151-54.

[25] Ibid.

[26] *Acts of Paul*, Hennecke, p. 357.

[27] *Acts of Paul*, ibid., p. 358.

[28] *Acts of Paul*, ibid.

[29] *Acts of Peter*, ibid., p. 317.

[30] *Acts of Peter*, ibid.

[31] See Leo Ferrero Raditsa, "Augustus' Legislation Concerning Marriage, Procreation, Love Affairs and Adultery," *Aufstieg und Niedergang der romischen Welt* 2.13 (1980):278-339.

[32] *Acts of Thomas*, Hennecke, p. 505.

[33] *Acts of Thomas*, ibid.

[34] Justin, *The Second Apology*, in *The Ante-Nicene Fathers*, vol. 1, ed. Roberts and Donaldson (Grand Rapids, Mich.: Wm. B. Eerdmans Publishing Co., 1950), pp. 188-89.

[35] Fischer, p. 263.

[36] See Sarah B. Pomeroy, *Women In Hellenistic Egypt from Alexander to Cleopatra* (NY: Schocken Books, 1984), pp. 3-40, and *Goddesses, Whores, Wives and Slaves* (NY: Schocken Books, 1975), pp. 121-25, on the Hellenistic queens; see Riet van Bremen, "Women and Wealth," *Images of Women in Antiquity*, ed. Cameron and Kuhrt (Detroit: Wayne State Univ. Press, 1983), pp. 223-42, on Hellenistic benefactresses; for a discussion of Roman women's political activities, see J.P.V.D. Balsdon, *Roman Women* (London: The Bodley Head, 1962), Judith P. Hallett, *Fathers and Daughters in Roman Society: Women and the Elite Family* (Princeton, NJ: Princeton Univ. Press, 1984), and Suzanne Dixon, "A Family Business: Women's role in Patronage and Politics at Rome 80-44 B.C.," *Classica et Mediaevalia* 34 (1983):91-112.

[37] This is the opinion of Averil Cameron, "Neither Male Nor Female," *Greece and Rome* (1980):60-68. Jo Ann McNamara, *A New Song: Celibate Women in the First Three Christian Centuries* (NY: Harrington Park Press, 1985), p. 66, suggests an alternative but not unrelated reason for the supposed predominance of women in early Christianity: in joining an unpopular and persecuted sect, women had less to lose than men.

[38] See Ross S. Kraemer, "Ecstasy and Possession: The Attraction of Women to the Cult of Dionysius," *Harvard Theological Review* 72 (1979):55-80; Pomeroy, *Goddesses*, pp. 217-26; Sharon Kelly Heyob, *The Cult of Isis Among Women in the Graeco-Roman World* (Leiden: E.J. Brill, 1975); Shaye J.D. Cohen, "Women in the Synagogues of Antiquity," *Conservative Judaism* 34 (Nov/Dec 1980):23-29; and Bernadette J. Brotten, *Women Leaders in the Ancient Synagogue* (Chico, CA: Scholars Press, 1982).

[39] Gerd Theissen, "The Sociological Interpretation of Religious traditions: Its Methodological Problems as Exemplified in Early Christianity," *The Social Setting of Pauline Christianity* (Philadelphia: Fortress Press, 1982), p. 188.

[40] Davies, *The Revolt of the Widows*, pp. 70-94.

[41] Jo Ann McNamara calls attention to this community of virgins with whom Antony left his sister, noting, "Clearly the history of the ascetic woman did not begin with Antony's flight"; *A New Song*, p. 1.

[42] *Acts of Thomas*, Hennecke, p. 475.

[43] Davies, p. 31.

[44] Ibid., p. 35.

[45] Ibid., p. 36.

[46] Ibid., p. 100.

[47] Ibid., p. 15.

[48] MacDonald, *The Legend and the Apostle*.

[49] *Acts of Paul*, Hennecke, p. 358.

[50] Bruno Bettelheim, *The Uses of Enchantment* (NY: Vintage Books, 1977), p. 94.

CONCLUSION

The chastity stories are historical sources. In the forego-
ing pages, we have tried to ascertain what historical knowledge can
and cannot be gleaned from these legendary texts and what
methodological approaches are appropriate to their study. Such
an attempt at methodological precision is required, for without it
these sources of women's history cannot be fully incorporated into
academic study of early Christianity.

But even when distilled to their most "historical" form, the
chastity stories offer more than a record of the past. They should
not be banished to the libraries of ancient historians. Like many of
the canonical stories, they communicate vividly across the ages
which separate us from their original tellers, offering us a means of
interpreting the present, and of giving shape to the future. In
concluding this study, we turn to a sociological evaluation of the
historical "data" collected in Chapter IV, considering whether and
how the history of the women behind the chastity stories offers a
positive model for Christian society.

Did the women behind the chastity stories find in Christianity a positive solution to their conflict with husbands and
patriarchal society? Or did Christianity have a neutral or even a
negative effect on the women's social position? The theoretical
model formulated by Gerd Theissen in his study of the sociological

functions of religion provides a helpful framework for considering these questions. Theissen maintains that religion has two main functions in social conflict, the restrictive and the creative. The restrictive function, which Theissen calls "compensation," is defined as the "suppression and illusory solution of conflicts"; the creative function, which he calls "innovation," is that which brings about the "actualization of potential for conflict."[1] Theissen is careful to point out that neither of these functions is theoretically positive or negative;[2] however, in this case, I identify compensation as a negative and innovation as a positive solution to the conflict experienced by women within the oppressive structures of patriarchal marriage. Thus, evaluating the social function of these stories and the Christian life style which they promote involves determining whether Christianity functioned as compensation or innovation for these women.

Theissen follows Marxist analysis in his description of the compensating function of religion:

> The compensating function of religious phenomena reveals itself cognitively in the devising of a counterpart to social reality, motivationally in the turning of existing impulses back onto replacement objects, emotionally in the discharging and dulling of social tensions.[3]

Many scholars would maintain that the new Christian life style chosen by the women who told the chastity stories was fundamentally compensating and represented no real social progress. Their arguments generally follow the lines of the two major subdivisions of the Marxist view of the compensating function of religion, the "opiate" theory and the "fetish" theory. According to the "opiate" theory, Christianity offers the promise of future blessedness in exchange for social progress in the present. In this function, Christianity produces social "drop-outs," who make no efforts to change worldly society, being convinced that they need only wait for the perfection of society in another world. The women of the chastity stories might be described as such "drop-outs," in as much as they withdraw from the social mainstream, and do so on the basis of their conviction that all worldly social institutions have been radically devalued in light of God's promise of eternal blessedness in heaven. Thus Mygdonia says to Marcia,

> May the remaining days of my life be cut short for me, mother, and may all the hours become as one hour, and may I depart from life, that I may go the more quickly and see that beautiful one whose fame I have heard, that living one and giver of life to those who believe in him, where there is neither day and night, nor light and darkness, nor good and evil, nor poor and rich, male and female, no free and slave, no proud that subdues the humble.[4]

Indeed, the women's renunciation of marriage and sexuality might be seen not only as "dropping out" of the fight for material progress, but as actual denial of those worldly pleasures they already possess in exchange for a heavenly reward. This is the view of Averil Cameron, who writes,

> The famous pronouncement, 'There is neither Jew nor Greek, there is neither bond nor free, there is neither male nor female; for ye are all one in Christ Jesus' (Gal 3.28) offers spiritual equality and the destruction of barriers, including sex barriers, through Christian baptism, but not worldly betterment . . . Ultimately women were to realize new potential only through *denying* their sex in the Christian idealization of virginity.[5]

G. E. M. de Ste. Croix comments in the same scriptural passage in similar fashion:

> [These passages] have a purely spiritual or eschatological meaning and relate only to the situation as it is 'in the sight of God,' or 'in the next world'; they have no significance whatever for this world, where the relations in real

life between man and woman, or master and slave, are
not affected in any way.[6]

Like Cameron, de Ste. Croix finds that Christianity not only fails to
bring about real change in the social position of women, but actually worsens their plight by upholding an "unhealthy attitude
toward sex and marriage,"[7] that is, by encouraging chastity.

While the general critique of early Christianity inherent in
these interpretations must be taken seriously, Christianity and
Christian chastity do not appear to serve a primarily compensating
function for the particular women who told the chastity stories.
Rather, the religious communities of women who told these stories
exemplify positive and creative social innovation.   The women
moved towards the creation of an alternative society based on a
radical transformation of social relationships, including the aboli-
tion of traditional sex roles and class distinctions.   While they
dropped out of a society which they found inadequate, they did not
drop out of social life altogether.   It is significant that the stories
they told were conversion stories which served to *introduce* an
alternative life style; the stories' ending is open, reaching out into
the future life of a community.[8] In this aspect they are to be contrasted with martyrdom stories, which conclude with death to the
world rather than with the building of a new society in the world.
Thus, it is not accurate to view the concerns of the women as
purely "otherworldly." The promise of a future state of blessedness
is the source of the women's courage and defiance.   However, their
eschatology is not purely futuristic.   It breaks into the women's
present lives dramatically.

Nor is women's sexual repression a purely negative factor
which represents a "trade-off" of present fulfillment for future reward.   Repression is not necessarily an "unhealthy" psychological
response.   Indeed, in a society in which sexuality is inextricably
linked with patriarchal marriage, sexual repression might be
viewed as a positive and liberating adaptation.   Scholars like de

Ste. Croix assume that sexuality is the essence of womanhood and that sexual repression is therefore by definition negative. Thus de Ste. Croix condemns both Christian marriage and chastity in the same breath, without noting the correspondence between the oppressiveness of marriage and the tendency to shun marriage:

> (1) As in Jewish marriage, the subjection of the woman to her husband was both more strongly emphasized than in other systems and given a divine origin not found elsewhere; and (2) an unhealthy attitude to sex and marriage can be seen in some books of the New Testament, regarded by the dominant form of early Christianity as divinely inspired, the very Word of God.[9]

A negative attitude toward sex and marriage might be a relatively "healthy" response to a marriage which strongly emphasizes the subjection of the woman to her husband. A positive expression of their sexuality does not seem to have been either an option or a particular concern for the Christian women who told the chastity stories.

The second theory of the compensating function of religion, the "fetish" theory, emphasizes that there is often a correspondence between social realities and religious ideas. This theory suggests that even in situations of social conflict, the compensating vision of an alternative "heavenly" society is, ironically, often a projection or a copy of the "worldly" society. Thus, some might claim that the Christianity reflected in the chastity stories simply substitutes the oppressive authority of God, Christ, or the apostles for the oppressive authority of the husbands and governors of the chastity stories. Ross Kraemer argues along these lines when she writes that although

> women are represented as rejecting their traditional sexual roles in the legends of ascetic Christianity, they are nonetheless still defined in terms of men, namely, the male divinity and his agent, the male apostle.[10]

This negative evaluation seems to rest on a false interpretation of the apostle's role. The apostle is a catalyst, a "donor," a temporary visitor in these stories, not a stable authority figure comparable to husband or governor. Nor do the women whose stories are celebrated represent religious authority within the community; with the possible exception of the Thecla story, the heroine is not elevated to a higher level, but is one member of a community, a character with whom the tellers and audiences are invited to identify. The only authority figure in the story is God/Christ, and the very absoluteness of the divine authority serves to relativize all human authority, and particularly all male authority. In reference to Jesus' command to "call no one father among you on earth for you have one heavenly father" (Mw 23.9), Elizabeth Schussler Fiorenza argues that

> The saying of Jesus uses the "father" name of God not as a legitimization for existing patriarchal power structures in society or church but as a critical subversion of all structures of domination. The "father" God of Jesus makes possible the "sisterhood of men" (in the phrase of Mary Daly) by denying any father, and all patriarchy, its right to existence. Neither the "brothers" nor the "sisters" in the Christian community can claim the "authority of the father" because that would involve claiming authority and power reserved for God alone.[11]

Similarly, one might argue that the chastity stories' depiction of Christ as "husband" or "lord" subverts the authority of any earthly husband or lord. The stories serve to diffuse rather than to legitimate human authority.

Christianity functioned creatively in its response to the conditions of social conflict in the lives of the women who told the chastity stories, insofar as it shaped a new community in which traditional sex roles and authority roles were abolished. The women and their communities and stories offer positive and inspiring social models and represent a part of Christian women's heritage which can be proudly claimed.

Notes

1 Gerd Theissen, "Theoretische Probleme religionssoziolog-ischer Forschung und die Analyse des Urchristentums," *Neue Zeitschrift für systematische Theologie* 16 (1974):42.

2 Ibid., pp. 55-56.

3 Ibid., p. 47.

4 *Acts of Thomas*, Hennecke, p. 511.

5 Cameron, "Neither Male Nor Female," p. 64.

6 G. E. M. de Ste. Croix, "Class, Exploitation and Class Struggle: Women," *The Class Struggle in the Ancient Greek World from the Archaic Age to the Arab Conquests* (Ithaca, NY: Cornell Univ. Press, 1981), pp. 107-8.

7 Ibid., p. 103.

8 See especially the ending of Maximilla's story, *Acts of Andrew*, Hennecke, p. 423, and of Mygdonia and Tertia's story, *Acts of Thomas*, ibid., p. 530.

9 de Ste. Croix, p. 103.

10 Ross Kraemer, "The Conversion of Women to Ascetic Forms of Christianity," *Signs* 6.2 (1980):303-4.

11 Fiorenza, *In Memory of Her*, p. 151.

APPENDIX:
SUMMARIES OF THE CHASTITY STORIES

The following summaries are based on the English texts in E. Hennecke, *New Testament Apocrypha*, vol. 2, ed. W. Schneemelcher, Eng. trans. ed. R. McL. Wilson (London: Lutterworth Press, 1965). Page references are to this edition; chapter references are to Hennecke's sources. For the *Acts of Andrew*, reference is also made to the recension of the story of Andrew's passion recently published by Theodore Detorakis in *Acts of the Second International Congress of Peloponnesian Studies* I (Athens, 1981-82), pp. 333-352.

1. *The Story of Agrippina, Nicaria, Euphemia, Doris, and Xanthippe*

(a) "And the concubines of the prefect Agrippa also came to Peter, being four in number, Agrippina and Nicaria and Euphemia and Doris. And hearing the preaching of purity and all the words of the Lord they were cut to the heart and agreed with each other to remain in purity (renouncing) intercourse with Agrippa; and they were molested by him. Now when Agrippa was perplexed and distressed about them--for he loved them passionately--he made inquiries, and when he sent (to find out) where they had gone, he discovered that (they had gone) to Peter. And when they came (back) he said to them, 'That Christian has taught you not to consort with me; I tell you, I will both destroy you and burn him alive.' They therefore took courage to suffer every injury from Agrippa, (wishing) only to be vexed by passion no longer, being strengthened by the power of Jesus." [*Acts of Peter*, pp. 316-17; *Act. Verc.* c. 33]

(b) "But one woman who was especially beautiful, the wife of Albinus the friend of Caesar, Xanthippe by name, came with the other ladies to Peter, and she too separated from Albinus. He therefore, filled with fury and passionate love for Xanthippe, and amazed that she would not even sleep in the same bed with him, was raging like a wild beast and wished to do away with Peter; for he knew that he was responsible for her leaving his bed. And many other women besides fell in love with the doctrine of purity and separated from their husbands, and men too ceased to sleep with their own wives, since they wished to worship God in sobriety and purity. So there was the greatest disquiet in Rome; and Albinus put his case to Agrippa, and said to him, 'Either you must get me satisfaction from Peter, who caused my wife's separation, or I shall do so myself'; and Agrippa said that he had been treated in the same way by him, by the separation of his concubines. And Albinus said to him, 'Why then do you delay, Agrippa? Let us find him and execute him as a trouble-maker, so that we may recover our wives, and in order to give satisfaction to those who cannot execute him who have themselves been deprived by him.' But while they made these plans Xanthippe discovered her husband's conspiracy with Agrippa and sent and told Peter, so that he might withdraw from Rome." But Christ appeared to Peter in a vision and told him not to flee. Peter was subsequently arrested and crucified. [*Acts of Peter*, pp. 317-22; *Act. Verc.* cc. 34-41]

2. *The Story of Maximilla*

[The first part of this story has not survived in its original form but can be reconstructed from later sources dependent on the *Acts of Andrew*]. Maximilla, wife of the proconsul Aegeates, was sick. Having heard of the arrival of the apostle Andrew, she sent her servant Iphidamia to beg Andrew to come visit her. When Andrew arrived, Aegeates was standing by his wife with sword in hand, ready to kill himself if his wife should die. Andrew rebuked Aegeates and healed Maximilla. [*Acts of Andrew*, content summary, pp. 400-3; *Acta Andreae Apostoli cum Laudatione Contexta* 33 and 38; Gregory of Tours, *Liber de Miraculis Beati Andreae Apostoli* 30; Epiphanius Monachus, *Peri tou biou kai ton praxeon kai telous Andreou* 24D-245B]

[From this point the story follows the extant text of the *Acts of Andrew*]. Subsequently, while Aegeates was absent in Rome, Maximilla again summoned Andrew, requesting that he heal a slave belonging to her brother-in-law Stratocles. Both Stratocles and the slave Alcman were converted, and Maximilla, Iphidamia, Stratocles and Alcman were baptized. The Christians gathered to worship with Andrew in Maximilla's bedroom.

Upon Aegeates' return, Maximilla escaped sexual relations with her husband by substituting a servant woman in his bed at night. Meanwhile, Maximilla visited Andrew every night. When Aegeates learned of Maximilla's deception and her visits to Andrew, he cruelly executed the slave woman who had pretended to be Maximilla and begged Maximilla to resume sexual relations with him. She refused.

Aegeates responded by seizing and imprisoning the apostle Andrew. Maximilla and Iphidamia sneaked away to visit the apostle in prison. According to a later source, an angel imitated their voices, "as if Maximilla were complaining about the suffering of the female sex and Iphidamia were answering her," so that Aegeates believed they were at home (*Acts of Andrew*, content summary, p. 403; Evodius of Uzala, *De fide contra Manicheos* 38). Aegeates threatened to kill Andrew if Maxmilla would not sleep with him. She and Iphidamia went again to visit Andrew in prison, and Andrew encouraged Maximilla to remain firm. Strengthened in her resolve, she returned to Aegeates and informed him of her decision never to sleep with him again.

Aegeates crucified Andrew, and Maximilla separated from Aegeates. "Aegeates urged her strongly [to return to him], promising her that she would have control over his affairs, but he was not able to persuade her. Than he got up one night exceptionally early and without any of his household knowing it threw himself down from a great height and died" (p. 416). The Christians were henceforth undisturbed. [*Acts of Andrew*, pp. 409-16, 423; *Cod. Vatic. Graec.* 808, cc. 3-18; *Narratio* 36-37]

3. The Story of Drusiana

(a) [The first part of this story, like the story of Maximilla, has not survived in its original form but can be inferred from references in the surviving text as well as from an account of the same story which is found in the fourth-century *Manichaean Psalm-Book*]. Drusiana's husband Andronicus, wishing to force her to abandon her vow of chastity, imprisoned her in a tomb; while she was imprisoned, the many-formed Christ appeared to her. Andronicus also imprisoned the apostle John at this time; he locked him up for fourteen days with the purpose of starving him to death. Both Drusiana and John were miraculously rescued, and Andronicus was converted. [*Acts of John*, content summary, p. 224]

(b) Sometime later, Callimachus fell in love with Drusiana, and in spite of the fact that Drusiana was both married and vowed to chastity, he boldly informed her of his desires. Drusiana was so disturbed by his overtures that two days later she took to her bed with a fever and died. Callimachus was undaunted. "Inflamed by the fiercest lust" (p. 247), he pursued her even into the grave. He bribed the steward Fortunatus and broke into the tomb, where he began to strip off Drusiana's grave-clothes.

At this moment a serpent appeared; it immediately killed the steward and then wound itself around Callimachus' feet. Callimachus either fainted or died from fright [the wording of the text is unclear]. The next day, John and Andronicus came to visit the tomb. They met a heavenly being at the doorway, and when they entered they found Fortunatus, Callimachus and the serpent lying on the floor. John raised Callimachus, who confessed what had happened and converted. Next, John raised Drusiana. Drusiana herself raised Fortunatus, but he did not repent and shortly thereafter died. John, Andronicus, Callimachus, and Drusiana celebrated the Eucharist together in great joy. [*Acts of John*, pp. 245-54; cc. 63-86]

4. The Story of Thecla

(a) When Paul arrived in Iconium, Thecla sat in a window for three days and nights without moving or eating and listened to his preaching. Her mother became concerned and sent for Thecla's fiance Thamyris. When Thamyris learned of Thecla's alarming behavior, he attempted to reason with her. But Thecla responded neither to him nor to her mother; she had ears only for Paul. Realizing that he had lost his beloved, Thamyris was filled with jealousy and rage. He convinced the city leaders and the Roman governor to imprison Paul, on the grounds that he was corrupting the women of the city. Thecla bribed the guard and joined Paul in prison. When she was discovered there, the citizens were outraged. Paul was scourged and driven out of the city, and Thecla was condemned to be burned. A vision of Christ in the form of Paul gave her the courage to face the ordeal. The fire was lit, but Thecla was miraculously saved when God caused rain and hail to quench the flames.

After her escape, Thecla sought Paul, and when she found him, she declared her desire to cut her hair and follow him. He hesitated: "The season is unfavourable, and thou art comely. May no other temptation come upon thee, worse than the first, and thou endure not and play the coward!" (p. 360). Thecla then asked him to strengthen her with baptism, but Paul told her to be patient.

(b) Paul and Thecla then journeyed to Antioch. Immediately, Alexander, a leading citizen, saw Thecla and fell in love with her. He tried to buy her from Paul, but Paul claimed that he did not know her. Then Alexander attempted to embrace Thecla, who resisted violently and humiliated him publicly. In his anger and shame, Alexander brought her before the governor, who condemned her to the wild beasts. During the fight, Thecla was miraculously saved four times. First a lioness defended her from a bear and a lion. When the lioness was killed, Thecla turned and jumped into a pool of water, baptizing herself in the name of Christ; she was saved from the vicious (?) seals in the pool when a bolt of lightning killed them. More beasts came, but the women from the crowd threw flowers and spices which drugged the animals. Finally, Thecla was tied to two fierce bulls. A protective flame blazed around her and burned through the ropes. At this point, Caesar's kinswoman the queen Tryphaena fainted out of fear for Thecla. Believing that Tryphaena was dead, the governor panicked and released Thecla, "lest the city also perish with her" (p. 363).

Once freed, Thecla stayed for some time with Tryphaena and taught her and her maidservants. But she yearned for Paul, so she dressed as a a man and went off in search of him, accompanied by a retinue of young women and men. When she found Paul, he was at first astonished, "pondering whether another temptation was not upon her." She explained all that had happened and announced that she was going to Iconium. Paul commissioned her : "Go and teach the word of God!" She spent the rest of her life teaching, "and after enlightening many with the word of God, she slept with a noble sleep" (p. 364). [*Acts of Paul*, pp. 355-64; *Acts of Paul and Thecla*, cc. 7-43]

5. The Story of Artemilla and Eubula

[This text is somewhat fragmentary and confused, but the story seems to read as follows]. In Ephesus, Paul had been condemned to the beasts by the governor Hieronymus. Eubula, the wife of one of Hieronymus' freedmen, was a disciple of Paul and sat with him day and night in prison. Her husband was jealous and hastened the proceedings for Paul's execution.

Meanwhile, Artemilla, Hieronymus' wife, asked Eubula to take her to Paul. The two women visited him in prison, and Artemilla requested baptism. That night Paul's bonds were miraculously loosed, and he left the prison with Artemilla to baptize her in the sea. During the baptism, Artemilla fainted [or died?] and Paul, with the help of the same heavenly being who had released him from prison, raised her. At dawn Paul returned to prison and sent Artemilla home.

Upon returning, Paul was immediately led to the beasts. Hieronymus, jealous and shamed by his wife's association with Paul, was present at the fight and ordered an especially fierce lion to be brought out. Artemilla and Eubula became dangerously ill through worry over Paul. But Paul was not killed. As it happened, the lion was one whom he had previously known and baptized. Together Paul and the lion fought off the other beasts, and they were aided by a hailstorm sent by God, which killed or wounded all present except Paul and the lion. Hieronymus' ear was torn off in the storm. Paul and the lion each escaped safely and went their separate ways. The women were relieved to learn of Paul's escape, and Hieronymus received a heavenly vision and was converted and healed. [*Acts of Paul*, pp. 370-73; PH, pp. 2-5]

6. The Story of the Princess Bride

A king heard of the wondrous powers of the apostle Thomas and commanded him to come and pray for his daughter and her new husband on the eve of their marriage. Thomas entered the bridal chamber, prayed, and departed, leaving the couple alone. But as the bridegroom túrned to embrace the bride , it appeared to him that she was still conversing with Thomas; actually, it was not Thomas, but Christ in the form of Thomas. Christ/Thomas taught the two through the night. When morning came, the king and his wife were amazed at the bride's boldness and lack of shame before her new husband. The bride explained: "I am no longer ashamed or abashed, because the work of shame and bashfulness has been removed far from me . . . . And that I have had no intercourse with a short-lived husband, the end of which is (remorse and bitterness) of soul, (is) because I am yoked with (the) true man" (p. 450). The bridegroom then admitted that he had likewise been converted to Christian chastity. The king was grieved and angry. He ordered that Thomas be brought to him and offered a reward for his arrest; but Thomas had already sailed away. Eventually, the bride and her husband and another Christian convert succeeded in teaching the king about the new faith. [*Acts of Thomas*, pp. 447-51; I.9-16]

7. The Story of Mygdonia and Tertia

(a) Mygdonia went to hear the apostle Thomas preach. After her first visit, she refused to dine or sleep with her husband Charisius; after her second, when he tried to force her, she resisted violently and fled from him naked; after her third visit, she cut her hair, rent her garments, and rejected Charisius utterly, in spite of his eloquent pleas of love. "He whom I love is better than thee and thy possessions" (p. 505), she declared. Meanwhile, Charisius convinced King Misdaeus, his kinsman, to imprison Thomas. Mygdonia and her maid Marcia sneaked out to meet the apostle, and he miraculously escaped prison and left for long enough to baptize the two women. Charisius then asked the king to release Thomas, hoping that if he did so, Thomas might convince Mygdonia to change her mind. Mygdonia, however, remained unswayed, and Charisius kept her locked up in the house.

(b) Tertia, wife of King Misdaeus, was sent to try to persuade Mygdonia to give in to Charisius, but when Mygdonia told Tertia about Thomas, Tertia decided to go herself to hear him speak, and she too was converted. The king was enraged and once again imprisoned Thomas.

(a-b) Next, Vazan, the king's son, went to visit Thomas in prison. Tertia, Mygdonia, and Marcia, all of whom had been locked up at home, escaped and joined Thomas in prison as well. Then the whole group left the prison to go baptize Tertia and Vazan. On their way, they met Mnesara, wife of Vazan, who had been miraculously healed; she too was baptized. Then Thomas, Mygdonia, Marcia, and Tertia all returned to their respective prisons.

The next day Thomas was put to death by King Misdaeus. "But Misdaeus and Charisius brought great pressure to bear on Tertia and Mygdonia, but did not persuade them to depart from their belief. And Judas appeared and said to them: 'Forget not the former things! For Jesus the holy and living will himself help you.' And those about Misdaeus and Charisius, being unable to persuade them, allowed them to live according to their own will" (p. 530). [*Acts of Thomas*, pp. 486-531; IX-XIII.82-170]

SELECTED BIBLIOGRAPHY

Primary Sources: Apocryphal Acts and Novels

Acta Apostolorum Apocrypha, ed. R. A. Lipsius and M. Bonnet, 2 vols. Hildesheim: Georg Olms Verlags-buchhandlung, 1959.

Acts of Andrew, ed. Theodore Detroakis. *Acts of the Second International Congress of Peloponnesian Studies* I. Athens, 1981-82. pp. 333-352.

Acts of Andrew, Acts of John, Acts of Paul, Acts of Peter, Acts of Thomas. E. Hennecke. *New Testament Apocrypha*, vol. 2, ed. W. Schneemelcher, Eng. trans. ed. R. McL. Wilson. London: Lutterworth Press, 1965.

Achilles Tatius. *Clitophon and Leucippe*, trans. S. Gaselee. Loeb Classical Library. NY: G. P. Putnam's Sons, 1917.

Chariton. *Chaereas and Callirhoe*, trans. W. E. Blake. Ann Arbor: Univ. of Michigan Press, 1939.

Heliodorus. *Ethiopian Story*, trans. W. Lamb. NY: E. P. Dutton & Co., 1961.

Longus. *Daphnis and Chloe. Three Greek Romances*, trans. M. Hadas. Indianapolis, NY & Kansas City: Bobbs-Merrill Col, Inc., 1953.

Xenophon. *An Ephesian Tale. Three Greek Romances*, trans. M. Hadas. Indianapolis, NY & Kansas City: Bobbs-Merrill Col, Inc., 1953.

The Hellenistic Novel and its Relation to the Apocryphal Acts

Dobschütz, Ernst von. "Der Roman in der alt-christlichen Literatur." *Deutsche Rundschau* 111 (1902):87-106.

Hägg, Tomas. *The Novel in Antiquity.* Berkeley & L.A.: Univ. of Cal. Press, 1983.

Kaestli, Jean-Daniel. "Les principales orientations de la recherche sur les Actes apocryphes des Apôtres." *Les Actes apocryphes des Apôtres,* ed. F. Bovon. Geneva: Labor et fides, 1981. pp. 49-67.

Kerenyi, Karl. *Die griechische-orientalische Romanliteratur in religionsgeschichtlicher Beleuchtung.* Tübingen, 1927. Reprint ed., Darmstadt: Wissenschaftliche Buchgesellschaft, 1962.

Perry, Ben Edwin. *The Ancient Romances: A Literary-Historical Account of Their Origins.* Berkeley & L.A.: Univ. of Cal. Press, 1967.

Rademacher, Ludwig. "Hippolytos und Thekla. Studien zur Geschichte von Legende und Kultus." *Sitzungsberichte, Kaiserliche Akademie der Wissenschaft in Wien, Philosophisch-historische Klasse* 182.3 (1916).

Reardon, B. P. "The Greek Novel." *Phoenix* 23 (1969): 291-309.

Reitzenstein, Richard. *Hellenistische Wundererzählungen.* Leipzig: B. G. Teubner, 1906.

Rohde, Erwin. *Der griechische Roman und seine Vorläufer,* 2nd ed. Leipzig: Breitkopf und Hartel, 1900.

Schneemelcher, W. and Schäferdiek, K. "Second and Third Century Acts of Apostles: Introduction." E. Hennecke. *New Testament Apocrypha,* vol. 2, ed. W. Schneemelcher, Engl. trans. ed. R. McL. Wilson. London: Lutterworth Press, 1965. pp. 167-88.

Söder, Rosa. *Die apokryphen Apostelgeschichten und die romanhafte Literatur der Antike.* Stuttgart, 1932. Reprint ed., Darmstadt: Wissenschaftliche Buch-gesellschaft, 1969.

Vielhauer, Philipp. "Apokryphe Apostelgeschichten." *Geschichte der urchristliche Literatur.* Berlin, NY: Walter de Gruyter, 1975. pp. 693-718.

Sociological Studies of the Apocryphal Acts

Davies, Stevan L. *The Revolt of the Widows: The Social World of the Apocryphal Acts.* Carbondale & Edwardsville: Southern Illinois Univ. Press, 1980.

Kraemer, Ross. "The Conversion of Women to Ascetic Forms of Christianity." *Signs* 6.2 (1980):298-307.

MacDonald, Dennis R. *The Legend and the Apostle: The Battle for Paul in Story and Canon.* Philadelphia: Westminster Press, 1983.

Folklore

Aarne, Antti and Thompson, Stith. *The Types of the Folktale.* Helsinkii Academia Scientiarum Fennica, 1961.

Bascom, William. "Four Functions of Folklore." *The Study of Folklore,* ed. A. Dundes. Englewood Cliffs, NJ, 1965. pp. 279-98.

Farrer, Claire R., ed. *Women and Folklore.* Austin & London: Univ. of Texas Press, 1975.

Fischer, J. L. "The Sociopsychological Analysis of Folktales." *Current Anthropology* 4.3 (June 1963): 235-95.

Honko, Lauri. "Methods in Folk-Narrative Research." *Ethnologia Europaea* 11 (1979/80):6-27.

Jordan, Rosan A. and Kalcik, Susan J., eds. *Women's Folklore, Women's Culture.* Philadelphia: Univ. of Penn. Press, 1985.

Propp, Vladimir. *Morphology of the Folktale,* 2nd ed. Austin: Univ. of Texas Press, 1968.

Thompson, Stith. *Motif-Index of Folk Literature.* Indiana Univ. Press, 1957.

Sociology

Theissen, Gerd.   "Theoretische Probleme religionssociologischer Forschung und die Analyse des Urchristentums."   *Neue Zeitschrift für systematische Theologie* 16 (1974):35-56.

INDEX

Achilles Tatius, 14, 45, 47, 50-51, 57, 65 n. 28, 66 n. 43, 70.

Acts of Andrew, 1, 3, 7, 35-36, 48, 58, 61, 67, 72, 89, 94, 95, 98, 99, 122-124.

Acts of John, 3, 7, 36-37, 61, 67, 99, 124-125.

Acts of Paul, 1-2, 3, 7, 37-39, 48, 49, 53-57, 58, 61, 67, 72, 76, 81, 88, 89, 93, 95, 98, 99, 101, 102, 105, 106, 125-127.

Acts of Peter, 1, 3, 7, 35, 61, 67, 72, 93, 99, 121-122.

Acts of Thomas, 3, 7, 39-40, 48, 61, 67, 72, 88, 94, 95, 99, 101, 115, 128-129.

Agrippina, 1, 3, 35, 61, 72, 121-122.

Andrew, 1, 35-36, 48, 72, 89, 122-124.

Apocryphal Acts, and the Hellenistic novel, 8-26; date and location of, 67; folklore origins of, 12-26; literary genre of, 8-26. See also: Chastity stories; *Acts of Andrew; Acts of John; Acts of Paul; Acts of Peter;* and *Acts of Thomas.*

Apostles, 42-44, 61, 62, 75, 87, 103-108, 118. See also: Andrew; John; Paul; Peter; and Thomas.

Artemilla, 3, 38-39, 61, 72, 88, 93, 99, 127.

Chaereas and Callirhoe: see Chariton.

Chariton, 44-45, 50-51, 52, 57, 65 n. 28.

Chastity stories, attached to martyrdom stories, 43-44, 58, 99-101, 116; compari-

son with Hellenistic novel, 48-57, 58-60, 105; folkloric origins of, 31-60; historical background of 87-109; narrative structure of, 34-35, 40-44, 62; summaries of, 121-129; variants of, 35-40, 57-58, 61, 121-129; women tellers of, 67-77.

Clitophon and Leucippe: see Achilles Tatius.

Daphnis and Chloe: see Longus.

Davies, Stevan, 76, 101, 103-104, 106.

Dobschütz, Ernst von, 8-9, 11, 14, 15, 16, 17, 21, 23, 24, 60.

Doris, 1, 3, 35, 61, 72, 121-122.

Drusiana, 3, 36-37, 61, 99, 124-125.

Ephesian Tale: see Xenophon.

Ethiopian Story: see Heliodorus.

Eubula, 3, 38-39, 61, 72, 94, 127.

Euphemia, 1, 3, 35, 61, 72, 121-122.

Folklore, as reflection of storytellers' world, 84-87; social and psychological functions of, 82-84; structuralist analysis of, 33-34, 40-43; tale types, 32-33, 49; women's, 68-77. See also: Apocryphal Acts, folkloric origins of; Chastity stories, folkloric origins of; and Novel, Hellenistic, folkloric origins of.

Heliodorus, 14, 45, 47-48, 65
    n. 28.
John, 36-37, 124-125.
Kaestli, Jean-Daniel, 21-22.
Kerenyi, Karl, 12-15, 16, 18,
    19, 20, 24.
Longus, 14, 45, 46, 52, 66 n.
    43.
MacDonald, Dennis, 22-23,
    25, 70-71, 105.
Maximilla, 1, 3, 35-36, 48, 58,
    61, 72, 89, 94, 95, 98, 99,
    122-124.
Mygdonia, 3, 39-40, 48, 61,
    72, 88, 94, 95, 99, 101,
    115, 128-129.
Nicaria, 1, 3, 35, 61, 72, 121-
    122.
Novel, Hellenistic, folkloric
    origins of, 12-26, 49-53,
    58; narrative structure of,
    48.   See also: Apocryphal
    Acts and the Hellenistic
    novel;   Chastity   stories,
    comparison with the Hel-
    lenistic   novel;   Achilles
    Tatius;   Chariton;
    Heliodorus; Longus; and
    Xenophon of Ephesus.
Paul, 1, 37-39, 48, 54-56, 72,
    76, 88, 89, 93, 105, 106,
    125-127.
Peter, 1, 35, 72, 121-122.
"Princess Bride," 3, 39, 61,
    94, 99, 101, 128.
Propp, Vladimir, 33-34, 40-
    43.
Rademacher, Ludwig, 12-13,
    14, 16, 18, 19, 22, 24.
Reitzenstein, Richard, 9-12,
    13, 16, 17, 18, 19.
Rohde, Erwin, 7-8, 13, 21, 25.
Söder, Rosa, 15-19, 20, 21,
    23-24.
Tertia, 3, 39-40, 61, 72, 94,
    99, 101, 128-129.
Thecla, 1-2, 3, 37-38, 48, 49,
    53-57, 58, 61, 72, 76, 81,
    89, 93, 95, 98, 99, 101,
    102, 105, 106, 125-127.

Theissen, Gerd, 113-114.
Thomas, 39-40, 48, 88, 128-
    129.
Vielhauer, Philipp, 19-20, 21.
Women, in community, 101-
    103, 116; in Hellenistic
    society, 68, 70-72, 77, 90-
    93, 100.   See also:
    Chastity stories, women
    tellers of; and Folklore,
    women's.
Xanthippe, 1, 3, 35, 61, 72,
    93, 99, 121-122.
Xenophon of Ephesus, 44, 45-
    46, 52-53.

STUDIES IN WOMEN AND RELIGION

1. Joyce L. Irwin, **Womanhood in Radical Protestantism: 1525-1675**

2. Elizabeth A. Clark, **Jerome, Chrysostom and Friends: Essays and Translations**

3. Maureen Muldoon, **Abortion: An Annotated Indexed Bibliography**

4. **Lucretia Mott: Her Complete Speeches and Sermons**, edited by Dana Greene

5. Lorine M. Getz, **Flannery O'Connor: Her Life, Library and Book Reviews**

6. Ben Kimpel, **Emily Dickinson as Philosopher**

7. Jean LaPorte, **The Role of Women in Early Christianity**

8. Gayle Kimball, **The Religious Ideas of Harriet Beecher Stowe: Her Gospel of Womenhood**

9. **John Chrysostom: On Virginity; Against Remarriage**, translated by Sally Rieger Shore

10. Dale A. Johnson, **Women in English Religion: 1700-1925**

11. Earl Kent Brown, **Women of Mr. Wesley's Methodism**

12. Ellen M. Umansky, **Lily Montagu and the Advancement of Liberal Judaism: From Vision to Vocation**

13. Ellen NicKenzie Lawson, **The Three Sarahs: Documents of Antebellum Black College Women**

14. Elizabeth A. Clark, **The Life of Melania the Younger: Introduction, Translation and Commentary**

15. **Lily Montagu: Sermons, Addresses, Letters and Prayers,** edited by Ellen M. Umansky

16. Marjorie Procter-Smith, **Women in Shaker Community and Worship: A Feminist Analysis of the Uses of Religious Symbolism**

17. Anne Barstow, **Joan of Arc: Heretic, Mystic, Shaman**

18. Marta Powell Harley, **A Revelation of Purgatory by an Unknown Fifteenth Century Woman Visionary: Introduction, Critical Text, and Translation**

19. Sr. Caritas McCarthy, **The Spirituality of Cornelia Connelly: In God, For God, With God**

20. Elizabeth A. Clark, **Ascetic Piety and Women's Faith: Essays in Late Ancient Christianity**

21. Carol and John Stoneburner (eds.), **The Influence of Quaker Women on American History: Biographical Studies**

22. Harold E. Raser, **Phoebe Palmer: Her Life and Thought**

23. Virginia Burrus, **Chastity As Autonomy: Women in the Stories of Apocryphal Acts**